HOW THE WEATHER WAS

How
the Weather Was

by Roger Kahn

HARPER & ROW, PUBLISHERS

New York
Evanston
San Francisco
London

Grateful acknowledgment is made for permission to reprint excerpts from the following:

Lines on page xii from "Once by the Pacific" and "Bereft," on page 94 from "The Secret Sits," on page 110 from "Precaution," on page 119 from "Reluctance," and on page 124 from "Sand Dunes" are from *The Poetry of Robert Frost* edited by Edward Connery Lathem. Copyright 1928, 1934, © 1969 by Holt, Rinehart and Winston, Inc. Copyright 1936, 1942, © 1956, 1962 by Robert Frost. Copyright © 1964, 1970 by Lesley Frost Ballantine. Reprinted by permission of Holt, Rinehart and Winston, Inc.

Lines on page 9 from "Nineteenth Century and After" are from *Collected Poems of William Butler Yeats*. Copyright 1933 by Macmillan Publishing Co., Inc. Renewed 1961 by Bertha Georgie Yeats. Reprinted by permission of Macmillan Publishing Co., Inc.

continued on following page

FIRST EDITION

Designed by Sidney Feinberg

Library of Congress Cataloging in Publication Data

Kahn, Roger.
    How the weather was.
    A selection of the author's profiles and articles from the world of sports, music, and literature.
    1. United States--Bibliography. I. Title.
CT220.K33   920'.073   73–4096
ISBN 0–06–012243–9

For Alice
Enchanting companion on these journeys

Contents

III Police Blotter

IV The Flower of the Field

Introduction:
Of Emperors and Clowns

The writer of books is at the mercy of forces over which he has little or no control: certain reviewers who—if they are not hostile—may not be qualified or objective; a public whose tastes and interests change as quickly as the weather; and a basic problem. Among contemporary American merits, bibliophilism finishes close to last.

If I know this now, I suspected it fifteen years ago. Indeed, the foreknowledge discouraged me from starting any serious books, and my experience with the first two, *The Passionate People* and *The Battle for Morningside Heights,* confirmed my suspicions. Fortunately, fairly early in my life at the typewriter, I was able to write for big magazines. No shark-toothed reviewers loitered there and, since magazines do not pay royalties, sales figures were someone else's concern. With diligence, which I possessed aplenty, and the right touch, I could reach great numbers of people and, from time to time, move some deeply. When I found this gift, magazine writing became not only a vocation but a passion.

Whenever I struck the right story subject, my response was intuitive and overwhelming. I felt a tightening of the solar

plexus. My heartbeat quickened. Then the slow unraveling began.

First, walk the paths of research. Find the man. Hear him out,
listening, as Detective Frank Lyons suggests, for the broken
rhythm that proclaims a lie. Listen for the defiant cadence of
truth. Then, when the research seems subdued and the note-
books are full, when the brain swells with fresh facts and churns
with unsuspected insights, walk to the chair, consider the desk
and face the typewriter.

For fifteen years, from the late 1950s into the 1970s, periodical
nonfiction was my uncertain ticket to immortality. Wanting
that ticket is why a man begins to write, or it had better be.
Writers need to believe in the future if they are to survive the
present.

At first, the periodical field looked bleak on sunny days. Certain of the successful magazines insisted on an optimistic, even
manic, view of life. These were *McCall's*, the *Saturday Evening
Post, Good Housekeeping*, the *Ladies' Home Journal*. In sum,
they comprised an American *Pravda*, which I took to calling
Superslick. It was rewarding to write for *Superslick*. The *Saturday Evening Post* offered good money for routine articles when
I was still an apprentice. But it was damnably hard to reach for
immortality in a magazine world where, as a point of policy,
readers were told that hard work always was rewarded, that no
one said shit, that casual seductions led to an early grave, that
good women found contentment drying dinner dishes, that
everybody was a WASP, that all Communists and many Demo-
crats were Satanic, and that Satan existed.

Ed Fitzgerald, who edited a small magazine called *Sport*,
encouraged a number of writers to publish seriously there and
in a companion magazine for men, called *Saga*. Much of *Saga*
described ministers playing dry variations on *Rain*, but that still
left room for occasional adult articles. Among *Saga*'s adventur-
ers and bawds, I published long and increasingly intense stories
about Frank Lloyd Wright, Jean Laffite, Jonas Salk and Garry
Davis, the world citizen.

Fitzgerald did not demand a pablum overview, nor did he superimpose stylistic oddities. Still, a *Sport-Saga* author faced certain drawbacks. There was no feedback from readers, and Fitzgerald's employers had wedged him between cost accountants. Before me lay a big, two-hearted world: pap, attention and Beef Wellington with the *Saturday Evening Post;* integrity, obscurity and stew meat with Ed Fitzgerald.

My first hope of a breakout was lit by a young editor at *Esquire*, named Clay S. Felker, who has since invented the magazine *New York*. Although I had neither met George Herman Ruth nor seen him swing a bat, Felker asked if I would set down Babe Ruth as he really had been. "Not a Boy Scout piece," Felker said. His smooth face formed a frown. He named an attractive price, and I prepared a Babe Ruth questionnaire. Bob Fishel of the Yankees found addresses for Ruth's surviving teammates. Since playing beside Ruth was the most dramatic aspect of many lives, the old ball players responded with great vitality. Soon I began to feel as though I knew "Jidge" Ruth well enough to admire, dislike and understand him.

Esquire declined to print my observation that Francis Cardinal Spellman's eulogy was tedious. Nor could I suggest, as had the Rabelaisian Jumpin' Joe Dugan, that the Ruth's so-called "bellyache heard 'round the world" was gonorrhea. Still, most of what I wrote was published. The story was chosen as E. P. Dutton's Best Sports Magazine Article of the year, and when I learned that Quentin Reynolds, a Dutton juror who'd known Ruth well, had composed an eighteen-page commentary extolling my sixteen-page article, tears filled my eyes and ran down my cheeks, drawing a sympathetic look from my first wife, and making me feel pride, embarrassment, surprise.

I approached Irving Goodman, who tended the Manhattan office of the *Saturday Evening Post.* I had written *Post* stories on horse races, air traffic controllers, actors. "Those were for them," I told Goodman. "Now I want to write one for myself."

"Such as?" he said, looking uncomfortable.

"Those visits. A reporter calls on Arthur Godfrey, and Godfrey chuckles. Let me go and call on a writer, a man who has something to say."

Goodman scowled. W. C. Heinz, a most distinguished crafts-man, had previously proposed that he visit his friend Ernest Hemingway at the Finca Vigía. This drew a classic, glacial re-sponse from the *Post*'s editorial board. "The *Saturday Evening Post* does not encourage articles about writers, particularly about writers whose work has never appeared in the *Saturday Evening Post.*"

"Who do *you* want to write about?" Irving Goodman asked.

"Robert Frost."

Goodman rubbed a stubbled chin. "I don't think they'd take a piece on poetry."

"Frost can talk about other things," I said.

"Give me a note," Goodman said. "Go light on the poetry."

I prepared a three-page letter, citing Frost on baseball, love, politics and disguising, or rather ignoring, his occupation. "They say okay, if you can bring it off," Goodman said in sur-prise a week later. "I only hope they mean okay."

Before driving to Ripton, I filled a stenographic notebook with questions. Some were broad. Can we discuss Freud and the way he seems to have affected writing? Marx? Joyce? Yeats young and Yeats old? Some were most specific. Can you remem-ber where you lived when you wrote:

> The clouds were low and hairy in the skies
> Like locks blown forward in a gleam of eyes.

Frost grumped at my opening pleasantries. In his weathered cabin he yawned and appeared distracted. I thought, I've taken him from his writing. I thought, I've taken him from poetry for a damn magazine piece. I thought, I've got to get the hell out of here. "Before I go, Mr. Frost," I began an unscheduled third question, "what I want to say is that a few lines in 'Bereft' mean a great deal. Where you write: 'Out in the porch's sagging floor/Leaves got up in a coil and hissed,/Blindly struck at my knee and missed.' I know the feeling, and what an image. Leaves as a snake. What an image."

Frost blinked alert. "You saw that," he said quietly. "Usually they only see what the anthologizers want 'em to see, but you saw that, did you? Very good." He tapped my arm in friendship and, without subsequently having to consult prepared questions, I spent a shining afternoon in conversation.

The *Saturday Evening Post* published the story along with a large photograph of Frost, peering across a tree branch. Within two weeks, I received three hundred letters. I had written my piece on my subject on my terms, and readers of the most prominent magazine in America were elated.

Mostly, *How the Weather Was* illustrates what happened after Babe Ruth and Robert Frost. I have since chosen to write only where the air looks clear, where a man can approach a story freely and write in any suitable style. Fortunately, *Superslick*'s hegemony faded during the 1960s. Steve Gelman appeared as articles editor of *Life* and financed my research into the anguishes of the great performers, Jascha Heifetz and Claudio Arrau. Otto Friedrich became managing editor of the *Saturday Evening Post* and worked a kind of magic on the fossil. Every issue of Friedrich's *Post* carried extraordinary writing. The economic forces that overwhelmed his and Gelman's enterprise worked their destruction beyond the editorial floors.

Versions of other stories were begun for *Esquire, The Nation, Sports Illustrated,* the Philadelphia *Inquirer,* wherever, as I say, the air looked clearest. But regardless of climate and freedom, serious writing for periodicals is contradictory. The medium is transient. I cannot imagine looking at old magazines, the *Post, The Nation* and the rest, as anything more than curios. They were prepared for shelf life of a week or two. And yet stories I wrote for these publications were intended for longer duration.

By increasing interest in my work through its popularity, *The Boys of Summer* has helped make possible *How the Weather*

Was. That kind of experience, writing a book out of internal drives and discovering that you have produced a best seller, is rich and strange and reminds a man that sunbursts still follow spring thunder, that beautiful women still say yes, and that books, unfettered by the demands of even the finest periodicals, are the best way for an author to bring his work before readers, now and in the future.

Although all but three of these stories were begun on commission from periodicals, the ensuing versions have been revised, restored and variously enlarged or trimmed to what seems a natural size. The exceptions are passages from *The Passionate People, The Battle for Morningside Heights* and *The Boys of Summer.* Even here, writing being a ceaseless process of revision, some editing has been done.

M. S. Wyeth, Jr., the executive editor of Harper & Row, was most helpful as I ingathered exile pieces; indeed, it was he who proposed the ingathering. I am particularly appreciative for his assistance across six months in defining a suitable range. But in the end, the range, like the style, reflects myself. Let the present, then, and the recent past, the ball players, poets, policemen, professors, musicians—in short, these emperors and clowns—stride before you, each hoping, as the author does, to please.

ROGER KAHN

Ridgefield, Connecticut
March, 1973

The good and the bad, the ecstasy, the remorse and sorrow, the people and the places and how the weather was. If you can get so that you can give that to people, then you are a writer.

ERNEST HEMINGWAY (to Carlos Baker)

I
The Metaphor
of Sport

*Not a matter of strikeouts, but
of people confronting fame and time
and themselves.*

Road Map

During the mauve years of Richard Nixon's vice-presidency, I served the hierarchy of a major magazine as sports editor. This was preferable to pederasty, although the distinction was not always clear.

My immediate superior had written sports in Bridgeport. There he learned to mistrust dialogue. "It makes for short lines," he complained, "and wastes space." *His* superior had published a sports magazine that failed. This man knew a number of anecdotes, which he habitually excised as stale, and did not know a number of others, which he excised as obscure. The executive editor was big, square, Yale and doggedly elitist. Finally, the editor himself indulged certain prejudices.

"Writing about niggers again, Kahn?" he said once.

"Look," I said. "It's my sports section."

"Yes," the editor said, "and it's my magazine."

As with cigarettes, the deleterious effects proceeded subtly, but when I left the magazine after four years, I found myself in agreement with an old *New York Times* sportswriter who liked to say, "Very little matters, and nothing matters much."

I contracted to rewrite a doctor's diet book; the chore consumed three weeks and produced a best seller. For no reason beyond vague curiosity about Hollywood, I ghosted Mickey Rooney's autobiography. We reaped large sums from editors who burned to know how the first Mrs. Rooney, Ava Gardner, behaved in bed.

Through these affluent, obscene, dissolute days, sports shone, and when Ingemar Johansson, the Göteborg Guggernaut, agreed to face Floyd Patterson for the third time, I got word to Stanley Woodward of the *Herald Tribune* that I would like to cover the fight and could work cheap. Woodward, an earth force disguised as a sports editor, said, "If you file a thousand words of notes and cover a dressing room, I'll pay you ten dollars."

In Miami Beach before the fight Max Schmeling strolled Collins Avenue to modest applause. Since Schmeling had represented Adolf Hitler as a paratrooper, the scene was troubling. "Of course Schmeling was not a Nazi," I explained. "As I get the picture, there were never more than six or seven Nazis in Germany. But they worked very hard." Then the sour memory of the mangling magazine editors charged to mind. Lufthansa, Volkswagen and the Argentine Tourist Bureau were advertisers. I placed the comment near the end of the notes.

After printing the entire story, Woodward sent a message saying that he had "liked the stuff enough to pay five times the agreed-upon price." With his $50 came an invitation for another drink.

I strutted into the Artist and Writers Restaurant. "Hello, Coach. Glad you liked the piece."

"Why did you bury the lead note?" Woodward growled.

"The Schmeling thing? I thought if you saw it you might kill it."

"You are a stupid son of a bitch," Woodward said, turning and showing a back that was broad as Asia. He would not speak to me for twenty minutes and I had to pay for my own Scotch.

As a writer I had tried to play the strumpet just a bit. This is as paradoxical as seeking to lose a rudiment of one's virginity. Certain things simply do not fraction. It struck me then that I had found out (and been found out) through sports. I have not since consciously buried a lead, nor have I ghosted a book, although on at least two occasions such books were offered for advances that ran into six figures.

From a distance, sports appear to be the shallow end of the American sea: puerile speeches at the letter-club banquet, the hustling of transparent con men, simple adults pursuing childhood activities, amiable anecdotes repeated on old-timers' day. The same man who demands harsh film criticism and likes his political reporting merciless accepts a pablum view of sport. He may find it sheer relief to turn to the sports page as a kind of toy department. He may have suffered from myopia at seven; in that case he enjoys putting down great hitters by pointing out that baseball is only a game.

Well, professional football is only a game. Its heroes drive forearms into throats at 4:15 P.M. They then kneel in group prayer at 4:20. No one who knows that should have been surprised when an Administration ruled by a football idolator ordered Cambodia invaded on a Thursday and proclaimed for that Sunday, "Let us pray."

Sports tell anyone who watches intelligently about the times in which we live: about managed news and corporate politics, about race and terror and what the process of aging does to strong men. If that sounds grim, there is courage and high humor, too.

In a sort of converse to the Woodward experience, I find sports a better area than most to look for truth. A great hockey goalie, describing his life on ice, once said, "That puck comes so hard, it could take an eye. I've had 250 stitches and I don't like pain. I get so nervous before every game, I lose my lunch."

"Some football players," I said to the goalie, whose name is Glenn Hall, "say that when they're badly scared they pray."

Hall looked disgusted. "If there is a God," he said, "let's hope he's doing something more important than watching hockey games." Offhand I can't recall a better sermon.

Without question we stand in the middle of a national sports boom. More teams. Greater attendance. Better athletes. Precisely where we stand in national sports journalism is less apparent.

The craft begins, I suppose, with Heywood Broun and Ring Lardner. What went before was anonymous and primitive. Broun is renowned for getting himself fired from the New York *World* when he would not stop defending the rights and subsequently the memories of Sacco and Vanzetti. He was happier playing right field in a Connecticut meadow.

Broun relished sport and he took football, baseball and boxing as frames on which to mount personal essays. A fight between a wild swinger called Rocky Kansas and the ultrasmooth Benny Leonard became a contest between Dada and tradition. At one point, Broun wrote, "Rocky Kansas partisans in the gallery began to split infinitives to show their contempt for Leonard and all stylists." I envy him a particular mix of metaphors: "The underdog can and will lick his weight in the wildcats of the world."

Lardner was cursed-blessed with genius. "His name was Francis X. Farrell," "Alibi Ike" begins, "and I guess the X stood for 'Excuse me.' " *You Know Me, Al* and its obscure sequel, *Lose with a Smile,* may be the only works of art built around American sport. "And," John Lardner said, proudly, "in both books what my father called a sun field really was a sun field and second base was always right where it belonged."

By contrast, Lardner's nonfiction suffers, but sometimes the shocking wit bursts through. He kept trying to see Georges Carpentier, a stylish Frenchman, who was training to fight the mighty Dempsey, and was put off three times with "M. Carpentier is sleeping." He then wrote, "Carpentier is practicing ten-second naps."

Like the present, the 1930s writhed with excess and sorrow.

Grantland Rice, the reigning sportswriter, was a lovely man who followed a flowery muse. His most famous story begins:

"Outlined against a blue-gray sky, The Four Horsemen rode again. In dramatic lore they are known as Famine, Pestilence, Destruction and Death. These are only aliases. Their real names are Stuhldreher, Miller, Crowley and Layden."

Rice was describing a fine Notre Dame backfield. Although the paragraph is a remarkable bit of work against a deadline, it is composed of a dangerous mix: fancy and overstatement. A Rice disciple, covering a football game at Annapolis in 1933, had poorer luck:

"Navy's ship of success foundered on the banks of the Severn today, wrecked by the rugged rocks of Pittsburgh. After a safe passage past Columbia, Penn State and Notre Dame abroad, the gallant craft came to grief at its home port, sunk by the waves of Pittsburgh's power."

Just about everything is wrong with that opening. It does not mention the sport, the crowd, the game, or the score, and the conceit is atrocious. For years this sort of prose raged on sports pages everywhere. "Miasma," Woodward called it.

Somehow, perhaps through the solemnity of World War II, sportswriting and the English language were reunited in the 1940s. Immediately, the craft flowered. Jimmy Cannon hewed his powerful, imagistic style. W. C. Heinz and later Ed Linn created a series of remarkable *verismo* magazine articles. A renegade English instructor, Joe H. Palmer, wrote marvelously about racing and its spas. Once Palmer defined a horse lover as "a horse which loves another horse." It is difficult to snatch epigrams from Red Smith's columns; the best are nearly seamless. Writing eight hundred words a day six times a week—"my daily spelling lesson," he said—Smith captured the fun of sport with endearing irreverence.

"Do you have any superstitions?" I asked him once.

"Only the Roman Catholic Church," Smith said. And, to reverse Maugham's mot, the man was the style.

Finally, tall, silent, bespectacled John Lardner guarded his family name and pride by writing a column for *Newsweek* once a week. "I couldn't make it right every day," he said. Listen to Lardner, circa 1957, discussing the dramatic one-punch knockout of Gene Fullmer by Sugar Ray Robinson in Chicago:

> An oddly shocking and confusing thing—neither good nor very bad, neither just nor very cruel—happened to Gene Fullmer, the young Mormon prizefighter in the boxing hall here the other night. When he went into the ring, his life was at its peak. He was famous, newly rich, powerful, confident, rising. A few minutes later he fell from power and glory to frustration and relative nothingness. And he cannot tell you from his own knowledge what happened. Not only power and glory are gone—the facts are missing, too. Thirty seconds of time, at the climax of his existence, are lost to him.
>
> To know what went on he has to be told. To believe it he has to look at a set of pictures. And this will be true for the rest of his life. It will be a strange, unsettling way to live.

For the right reader at the right time these lines transcend sport. They ask how many of us have been unconscious, or at least unaware, as the most important event in our life passed quickly by.

Al Silverman, who as editor of *Sport* magazine had to purchase a dozen articles every month, suggests that we are in the age of the chipmunk. A chipmunk is a hard-working reporter who asks impertinent questions, is not obsessed with protecting his sources, and scurries about for stories like a—well, chipmunk. "The Selma of the chipmunk movement," Silverman says, "was the World Series of 1962. Our magazine gave Ralph Terry a car for beating the Giants twice. His wife called him in the Yankee dressing room to congratulate him and say the new baby was coming along fine.

" 'Where's your wife?' a reporter asked.

" 'Feeding the baby,' Terry said.

" 'Breast or bottle?' asked the reporter.

"Terry answered the question and that epitomizes the chipmunk approach and the interesting climate it creates."

Silverman's cheer at chipmunks, while remembering lions, is an emotion previously described:

> Though the great song return no more
> There's keen delight in what we have:
> The rattle of pebbles on the shore
> Under the receding wave.

I don't suggest that sportswriting in the 1950s was uniformly good. Much was dreadful. Nor do I demean chipmunks and other craftsmen: Maury Allen, Stan Isaacs, Vic Ziegel, to name three chipmunks; Dick Young of the *Daily News*, a remarkable advocacy journalist; Jim Murray of Los Angeles, Jack Murphy of San Diego, John Owen of Seattle, Wells Twombly of San Francisco and Arthur Daley, whose column in the *New York Times* glows with the amiability of the man. We have, however, been considering giants in their prime. Now one finds none.

Woodward and Lardner have died. Heinz and Linn write novels. For many years, Cannon and Smith were shut out of New York by the storms that have assaulted journalism. We have lost not only remarkable men but institutions that supported remarkable men.

The old *Collier's* published an unusual variety of sports articles. Once the magazine employed a physicist who could affix a kind of speedometer to baseball bats. Athletes and an essayist were hired, and presently we had stylish, scientific proof: Theodore Bernard Kluszewski, who cut his uniform sleeves at the shoulder to provide aeration for his biceps, possessed the hardest swing in baseball. There was barely time to celebrate this journalistic enterprise before *Collier's* collapsed.

The *Saturday Evening Post* entered the twentieth century during 1961, and the sporting manifestation of this time warp sparkled in a hundred issues. *Post* writers, or authors, as the magazine's executives preferred to call them, had suffered decades of sophomoric editing. As one author, the late Al Hirsh-berg, put it, "To sell the *Post*, you write a nice bright piece and then you dull it up a little." Abruptly, the *Post* tolerated and even encouraged brightness. A man could write as well and as powerfully as he knew how, and he could almost (but not quite) quote athletes as they spoke. This time the celebrations had a longer run. The *Post*—the serious, important, vibrant *Post*—endured for seven years.

Look died. *Life* died. Thirty or forty newspapers have folded since the fifties. From my own aerie in Connecticut I share with Marcuse and Agnew a horror of monopoly journalism.

When nine men covered Ted Williams, it was impossible to conceal the fact that Williams, while an astonishing batsman, was a pill. If one writer courted The Thumper by refusing to report a tantrum, another inevitably seized the tantrum as news. Williams would then speak to neither, until he needed a favor. Regardless of each reporter's skill, an essential, imperfect system of checks and balances worked. If you cared enough about Williams, and I did, you could find a portrait that was honest by consensus.

Sports books have grown increasingly more mature than they were in the days when each was dismissed with an editor's avuncular "Now remember, we're aiming for young adults, say twelve to fifteen." But books properly are a reflective form; for reasons that range from art to production schedules, reporting so-called hard news remains somebody else's business. Which leaves us with the opiate of the new masses.

As the media men say, TV makes every living room an arena. If that's what you want for your living room, televised sport can be thrilling. A good director shows aspects you cannot see on scene: lips moving in profanity, a winner's glower, a loser's tears. But TV confuses people by forever mixing the true with the false. "Watch this on instant replay; see how the pitcher winces." And a moment later the same voice: "Glooble Beer will help you lose weight. And say, girls, it's also an excellent depilatory."

"Trivia," Otto Friedrich sniffs at sport in *Decline and Fall,* but clearly sport is significant. It is big business and that matters and it is a theater of truth and it holds up a mirror to society and humanity.

Willis Reed, a gigantic black of Bernice, Louisiana, and New York, is not only captain of the Knickerbockers but the team leader and protector. When someone turned on Bill Bradley, Reed informed the aggressor: "I'm king here. If any asses get kicked in, I do the kicking." Bradley, W.A.S.P., Princeton, Rhodes Scholar, was a happy member of King Willis' court.

Two members of the St. Louis football Cardinals confessed that they had joined the SDS. One described professional football in terms of society. "The structure is reactionary. We live in a goddamn military camp. The shit comes down from above."

The old Dallas quarterback Don Meredith has cried out against the duality of life. "I couldn't be somber," he told Gary Cartwright, "but some players didn't understand this. They thought I was unconcerned. I had to pull away. I'm naturally gregarious, but, ensign, it's a lonely life there on the bridge."

Sports is about people who are inner-directed, outer-directed, nondirected and omni-directed. Frank Ryan, topologist, Ph.D., assistant professor of mathematics at Case Western Reserve, signed on at thirty-four to be substitute quarterback in Washington. A black outfielder, Curt Flood, lost income and shortened his career by challenging the legality of baseball's standard player contract. In a basketball dressing room, on a night when fans have jeered Lew Alcindor, now Kareem Abdul-Jabbar, Alcindor's father considers a deeper cruelty. After four years at Juilliard, Alcindor père, a trombonist, was barred from orchestras because he is black.

"I get more work now," he says, "but it is too late to make a living at it. Berlioz is my favorite."

"The *Requiem?*"

"*Symphonie Fantastique.*"

All around basketball players discuss pick-off plays. Mr. Alcindor discourses on trombones in Berlioz. The sports scene is forever surprising, forever fresh, forever forcing a kind of honesty, which leads back to our starting place.

After quitting the magazine job, I ran with Vic Obeck, a genial man who had been a professional football player. We were leaving the dining room of Toots Shor's restaurant one night when Richard Nixon waved from a corner. He was out of office then and waving at everyone.

"Let me handle this," I said. I strode to Nixon's table and, with the fierce courage of whiskey, introduced myself, said we knew each other and sat down. Nixon smiled greenly. Several lawyers in his party glared.

"I wonder if you'd say hello to an admirer of yours, who is athletic director up at NYU?"

"Of course," Nixon said through the green smile.

"Hey, Vic," I shouted, rising. "Come on over and meet my friend Dick Nixon."

"What else should I know about him?" Nixon said urgently.

"Guard. Football Dodgers. 1946. Good blocker."

Nixon's head jerked in a nod. "Vic," he began, "I'm really pleased to shake your hand and we were just wondering here why the city doesn't do more for NYU sports. They ought to build a new basketball arena."

Obeck beamed.

"I remember you with the old Brooklyn football Dodgers," Nixon said.

"Really?" Obeck was a political conservative and his eyes became so bright that I was afraid he might weep.

"Yes, sir," Nixon said, "you were a great blocker. I'll never forget the way you blocked for Ace Parker."

The bright eyes glazed. Ace Parker played in the 1930s. Obeck blocked for a passer named Glenn Dobbs. In sport, as in Watergate, the blunderer gives himself away.

the writers who traveled with him or the fans who watched him; even more clearly, perhaps, than the women—the adopted daughters and the wife—who loved him most. For they knew him in the camaraderie of strong, successful men, where no man passed verdict on the other but where everyone knew "Jidge" Ruth was at once the strongest and most successful.

There is a curious derivative of Gresham's law that applies to American heroes. Just as bad money drives out good, so heroic fancy drives out heroic fact, and we are often left standing in a forest of chopped-down cherry trees wondering what our man actually was like. The greater the hero, the more prevalent the fictions. Since Ruth was the most popular of baseball heroes, movie companies, careless writers and glib storytellers have busied themselves with the obfuscation of fact.

But to begin with, everything you have ever heard about Ruth on a baseball field is probably the truth or close to it. Ruth could hit a baseball higher, farther and more dramatically than anyone else. His record of 60 home runs in one 154-game season is unquestionably the classic of all sports standards. His career totals of 714 home runs and 2,056 bases on balls stood beyond challenge for thirty years. His great swing, even when he struck out, was more awesome than the stroke of a lesser man which happened to produce a home run.

He probably did, as he claimed, call his shot against the Chicago Cubs in the 1932 World Series, when with two strikes he pointed toward the bleachers, then whaled the next pitch where he had pointed. Wally Pipp, one of Ruth's old teammates, explained that whenever Ruth was sure of himself and on a spot, he held up the first two fingers of his right hand to let the pitcher know that there was still one strike left, which would be enough. But others who were there say the Chicago gesture was unmistakable, so the incident well may have transpired as Ruth told it.

He does seem always to have made the right play in the outfield. He did have superlative baseball instincts. He did

A Look Behind
a Legend

In his time and in his way, George Herman Ruth was a holy sinner. He was a man of measureless lust, selfishness and appetites, but he was also a man undyingly faithful, in a manner, to both his public and to his game. Tradition, which always distorts, remolded Ruth as extensively in a quarter-century as it remolded Abraham Lincoln in a hundred years. Just twenty-five years after his death and thirty-eight years after his last disastrous season, only the image of holiness remains.

Ruth died on August 16, 1948. After the funeral service, as a great crowd stood in reverent silence, pallbearers, many of them Ruth's own teammates, carried the casket into the fierce heat of the summer day.

"Lord," whispered Joe Dugan, the Yankee third baseman during Ruth's prime, "I'd give my right arm for an ice-cold beer."

Waite Hoyt, the former pitcher, grunted under the burden of the coffin and turned slightly. "Joe," he murmured, "so would the Babe."

The middle-aged men who spent their youth playing side by side with Ruth remember. They remember more clearly than bring all players' salaries up behind his own and, more assuredly than anything else, he was the savior baseball had to find after the Chicago White Sox dumped the 1919 World Series. All these are part of the legend, and all ring true.

But once the stories of Ruth move off the diamond, fact fades away and dies. He liked children, but his life was not a priestly dedication to healing sick boys. He liked jokes, but his humor at best was coarse. He was devoutly religious, but only sporadically, when suddenly he felt compelled to make up for lost time in church. He may not have been an utter social boor, but he was something less than tactful, something less than gracious, something very much less than sensitive.

Once when he accidentally spiked a Yankee named Ray Morehart, he apologized profusely, then said to a veteran, "Hey, when that guy join the club? Last week?" Morehart had been with the club for months. Ruth hadn't noticed. To him everyone under thirty-five was "Kid" and everyone older was "Doc." He was absorbed in himself and his talent and, although he was generous with audiences to fans, these were never anything more than audiences. Fans came to Ruth. Celebrities came to Ruth. The world came to Ruth. Ruth went to no one, unless summoned.

What was he like? Bennie Bengough, the old catcher, remembered that in his own rookie year of 1923, Ruth, the veteran, made a point each payday of displaying his paycheck from the Yankees. "Hey, kid," he'd say to Bengough. "Hey, Barney Google. How'd you like to have this, kid?" Each two-week check was for $2,000, which Bengough said was more than he earned all year. "But," Bengough added, "he didn't show it in a boasting way. More like it was his idea of fun."

Dugan was already established as a star when the Yankees acquired him from the Boston Red Sox that season. On the day Dugan joined the club, Ruth dumped a batch of mail in his lap. "Open these for me, will ya, kid?" Ruth said. "Keep the ones with checks and the ones from broads. Throw out the others."

It was just before game time and Ruth, following his custom, was late. He undressed quickly while Dugan went through one pile of mail and Whitey Witt, the center fielder, went through another.

"Here's a wire from Ziegfeld," Witt said. "He'll give you fifteen hundred bucks a week to go in a show next winter."

Ruth crumpled the wire and threw it away. "I ain't an actor," he said.

"Christ," said Mike McNally, a reserve infielder, "make it while you can. For fifteen hundred a week, learn to act."

"Yeah," Ruth said, putting on his spikes. "Yeah."

"If you go in a show," McNally said, "and I come into town to see you, can you get me a couple of Annie Oakleys?"

"If I go in a show, I'll get you guys all the broads you want."

Babe Ruth, a huge, ignorant, sentimental emperor, was the product of a childhood so bleak that it was almost no childhood at all. Then, in his early manhood, he found himself earning considerably more money and possessing far more popularity than the President of the United States. He was not humble in his change of fortune. He knew that he was the biggest name in baseball, and whatever his skill brought him, he not only accepted but demanded.

Once when he visited France, accompanied by his wife and daughter, he surprised Americans who knew him well by announcing, "Paris ain't much of a town." Parisian crowds had failed to recognize him. The American Embassy there, receiving a letter addressed to George Herman Ruth, took an advertisement in the Paris *Herald Tribune* listing Ruth's name along with many others found on unclaimed mail. "How do you like them guys?" Ruth said in anger and in pain. "Taking an ad in the paper to find out where the hell I am! That could never happen in New York."

It never could have. Ruth lived for fifty-three years, but his special time was the fifteen seasons he played for the New York Yankees. In the twenties, the country teemed with sports figures whose names meant immediate idolatry: Tilden and Grange, Rockne and Dempsey, Ty Cobb and Bobby Jones and John McGraw. No one gathered and awed so many crowds for so many years as the man the whole nation called "The Babe."

On the field, his shape was unique. It was thick through the shoulders, prodigious at the belly and set on comically thin legs. He was pigeon-toed and he ran with delicate, mincing steps that all but concealed his speed. Off the field the man had other marks. He chewed cigars and wore camel's-hair polo coats and affected a light-brown cap. His face was broad and wide, dominated by a vast, flat nose and an overhanging brow. His voice was hoarse and loud. As he moved, center stage moved with him.

Ruth appeared on the American scene through the modest gateway of Baltimore, Maryland, where he was born in 1895, one of the number of children with which the union of Kate Schanberg and G. H. Ruth, Sr. was blessed. In later years, Ruth invariably claimed that his father owned a saloon and that he had been born a few flights above the bar. This is open to serious question. Photographs of Ruth's birthplace show no ground-floor saloon, only the inevitable Baltimore white stoop-front. Undoubtedly, the elder Ruth was familiar with Baltimore saloons, but whether as entrepreneur or client remains uncertain.

Like W. C. Fields, Babe Ruth never tasted liquor before he was six. He also chewed tobacco and appears to have stolen whatever loose change his parents left about the house. "I was a bad kid," Ruth himself said afterward. In 1902, when he was seven, Ruth was placed in St. Mary's Industrial School as an incorrigible. He was not, of course, an orphan, as legend insists. He was the unmanageable child of parents who were not passionately dedicated to parenthood.

St. Mary's, a pile of masonry as solemn as a prison, was fenced off from the outside world and run by the Roman Catholic Order of Xaveran Brothers. There, under the guidance of Brother Matthias, a gentle man six and a half feet tall, Ruth was taught to read and to write, schooled in the crafts of tailoring and shirtmaking and, in his spare hours, he played baseball. No one ever had to teach him baseball. Ruth was the ultimate natural. At nineteen, St. Mary's released him to the Baltimore Orioles, who were then in the International League, and, staggered by a $600-a-year contract, Ruth went forth into the world. He was a babe; the nickname came quickly and logically.

Within two seasons he was starring as pitcher and pinch-hitter for the Red Sox. In eight matches with Walter Johnson, the finest of modern American League pitchers, Ruth won six, three by scores of 1 to 0 and once when his homer provided the only run. In World Series competition he pitched twenty-nine consecutive scoreless innings. Ruth was a superb left-hander. He chose to move into the outfield for Boston in 1919 only because his pinch-hitting was so effective that he could earn more playing every day.

In 1920 the Yankees purchased Ruth for $100,000. Colonel Jake Ruppert, one of the owners, had to take out a $370,000 mortgage on Fenway Park, the Red Sox's field, as the second provision of what was the biggest of baseball deals up to that time. Dividends were prompt. In his first season with the Yankees, Ruth hit fifty-four home runs, almost double the old record and an achievement beyond belief to fans accustomed to home-run champions with totals of ten or twelve. Abruptly, Ruth was the wonder of baseball. The fans recognized it and so did Ruth.

This, then, was his stage:

An incredulous, idolizing America, gaping through the twenties, and all the while congratulating itself on its own maturity.

Here were the supporting players:

Jumping Joe Dugan, out of Holy Cross. Intelligent, quiet, gifted. Could take a drink.

Waite Hoyt, high-school graduate, who later attended a school for undertakers. Acerbic, witty, skilled. Could take a drink.

Miller Huggins, manager. Diminutive old baseball pro. Acid, tough and unamused by jokes about his size. Could take a drink, but preferred his players not to.

Bob Meusel. Tall, silent. Could take a drink.

Whitey Witt. Short, garrulous. Could take a drink.

Assorted other players, courtesans, lords, ladies and presidents.

This is what he did:

Led the American League in homers every year but one in the decade.

Led the Yankees into seven World Series.

Drew a salary that went in rapid stages to $52,000 to $70,000 to $80,000.

Provided the gate appeal that created Yankee Stadium.

Rebuilt the game, which had been scientific, into an extension of his own slugging style.

And this is how he played his role:

One day in 1924 (forty-six homers for The Babe) Herb Pennock, a genteel pitcher, was asked to attend a party sponsored by a prominent family near Wilmington, Delaware. "Hug," Pennock said, "they want some Yankees; I need two dozen autographed balls and three players."

"You got the balls," Huggins said. "Which players?"

"Ruth, Dugan and Meusel."

"Okay," Huggins said, "but remember. We got a game in Philly tomorrow."

Ruth was the hit of the party. Yes, he said, baseball had come easy to him. The swing? Well, he'd liked the way Shoeless Joe Jackson used to swing and maybe he kinda copied Jackson's wrist action. That guy swung good. Later, after hours of drinking and baseball talk, Ruth grew bemused and set out for a brunette, who, it developed, was one of the maids.

"Babe," said a boxing promoter from Philadelphia, "you got to get outa here."

"Not without that broad," Ruth said.

"Come on," said the boxing man, "I'll get you broads in Philly better than her."

"You sure?" Ruth said.

In Philadelphia, the boxing man took Ruth to a building in which he was absolutely certain they would find girls. Hours later, as dawn appeared over eastern Philadelphia, the boxing man suggested that Ruth leave. Ruth was sitting in an easy chair, a girl on each knee. He held an open bottle of champagne upside down over his head. "I ain't gonna be leaving for a while yet," Ruth said.

At Shibe Park that afternoon, Ruth, who may not have slept, announced, "I feel real good."

"You don't look real good," said Fred Merkle, a National League veteran who was finishing his career with the Yankees.

"I'll hit one," Ruth said.

"Bet?" Merkle said.

"A hundred," Ruth said.

"Wait a minute," Merkle said. "This is an easy ball park."

"All right," Ruth said. "I'll give you two-to-one."

On his first time at bat, Ruth walloped an outside pitch into the left-field stands and won his bet. Then he lined a triple to right, crashed a triple over Al Simmons' head in center and pulled a homer over the right-field wall. He had gone four for four, with two triples and two homers, without benefit of bed rest.

One day in 1927 (sixty homers and $70,000) Ruth played golf at a course near Scarsdale, New York. Ruth drove long and well, as he generally did, but his putting was terrible. After nine holes, he diagnosed the difficulty. "Them goddamn squirrels running in and outa the trees," he said. "They're killing my game."

"It isn't the squirrels," Joe Dugan said.

"Kid," Ruth said to his caddie, "get me an air rifle."

"There isn't one around," the caddie said.

"Get one for The Babe," Ruth said.

Presently the caddie found a .22-caliber rifle and a handful of shells. "Now," Ruth said, "we're gonna fix 'em."

He loaded and began picking off squirrels as easily as he picked off fast balls. "Mr. Ruth, Mr. Ruth," shouted the club pro, who had come running at the sound of gunfire, "you'll have to stop that. You're endangering our members."

"Just a couple more," Ruth said, "and I'll be going."

That night in his suite at the Hotel Ansonia on Broadway, Ruth cooked a squirrel potpie. "Did you ever taste squirrel potpie?" Dugan asks. "Hell, I couldn't eat for a week."

One day in 1928 (fifty-four homers and $70,000), it came up rain at Yankee Stadium and Ruth, who had spent the morning waiting for the rain to stop, grew bored. "What are we gonna do?" he asked Hoyt. "Let's get drunk."

"Not me," Hoyt said. "I pitch tomorrow."

"Joe?" Ruth said to Dugan.

"Let's go out to the track," Dugan said.

Ruth bet $500 across the board, a total of $1,500, on a steeplechase horse that had caught his fancy. The horse fell at the first jump. "You Irish son of a bitch," he roared at Dugan. "You shanty bastard. We coulda been drunk for six weeks on the dough I dropped." Before the afternoon ended, Ruth recouped. "Come on, Joe," he said. "You had a helluvan idea. I'm gonna throw you a party soon as we get back."

To George Herman Ruth, women, money and liquor were equally important. They were necessities which he took for granted. In 1915, his first full year with the Red Sox, he married a Nova Scotia girl named Helen Woodring, but a few years later they separated. The first Mrs. Ruth died in a fire in 1929. Ruth then married a former actress named Claire Hodgson, whom he called Clara and to whom, despite her continual efforts to tame him, he remained deeply attached. Still, Ruth was more than a two-woman man.

"Every spring," says one old Yankee, "he used to hand me a

hell of a laugh. We'd play in one town after another in the South and whenever the train pulled out of the station, there'd be a half-dozen girls waving good-bye to him. 'Good-bye,' the big guy would say real sweet. 'See you next year, girls.'

"One year it caught up with him. He collapsed on the field, all doubled over, and the club had to put out a story that he'd eaten a dozen hot dogs and drunk a couple dozen bottles of soda pop. He was real sick and it made a lot of headlines. 'The bellyache heard round the world,' the writers called it. Well, Ruth hadn't been drinking that much pop, and it wasn't even a bellyache. It was something a little bit lower."

Until Whitey Witt left the club after the 1925 season, he roomed with Dugan and the two had a standing invitation to join Ruth in his suite early any evening. It was always the same. Cases of good bootleg liquor were piled in the bathroom, and a keg of beer stood in the tub. When the phone rang, Witt was expected to answer.

"Tell her to come up," Ruth would shout. "Tell her I'm glad to see her."

By midnight Ruth would have made his selection from the available entries. "Good night," he'd tell Dugan and Witt, who would then leave in a swirl of rejected applicants.

In the course of this existence, money was a casual thing, except during the late winter, when Ruth negotiated his contract with Ruppert. Overall, Ruth earned $1,076,474 from baseball. No one, least of all Ruth, ever calculated what he earned from ghost-written articles, personal appearances and endorsements. The generally accepted figure is $1,000,000, and it must stand.

One April, when he was earning $70,000 a year, Ruth found himself without funds to pay his income-tax bill, which in those laissez-faire days was $1,500. Hoyt and Dugan each put up $750, and Ruth paid the tax.

A month later Ruth approached with a bankroll. "I wanna give you six percent," he said. "You guys figure it out."

"Six percent," Hoyt said, shocked.

"What the hell do you think we are," Dugan said, "taking interest from a teammate? Just what we lent you, Jidge. No more."

It was some time before the two convinced Ruth that the loan was a favor, not a business transaction. Later, on a Western trip, Dugan found himself strapped before a dinner date in Cleveland. Ruth was talking to tourists in the hotel lobby, and Dugan walked up quietly and said, "Jidge, I am empty-handed."

Without looking, and without interrupting his conversation, Ruth pressed a bill into Dugan's palm. Dugan pocketed it, also without looking, and when the check was presented in the restaurant, he handed the borrowed bill to the waiter.

"You kidding, mister?" said the waiter, who looked.

"What?"

"I can't change it. Come on, gimme a twenty."

Dugan examined the money. It was a $500 bill. Soon after as the Yankees returned to New York, he gave Ruth a $500 check.

"What the hell is this?" Ruth asked.

"The dough you lent me in Cleveland," Dugan said.

"Christ," Ruth said, "I thought I blew it."

Ruth apparently never voted in an election until 1944, when, moved by opposition to a fourth term for Mr. Roosevelt, he registered, took a literacy test and passed. But without benefit of voting, he was actively interested in the 1928 campaign of Al Smith, who, like Ruth, was a Roman Catholic. Ruth organized a political-action group called "Yankees for Smith," which was effective in a limited way.

During the early stages of the 1928 race, Herbert Hoover, as all presidential candidates, became a politic baseball fan. During one of his trips to Griffith Stadium, he decided a picture with Ruth might be in order. One of the Yankees overheard a Washington official discussing the plans and tipped off Ruth, who then remained in the clubhouse until game time. "I ain't gonna pose with him," Ruth said. "I'm for Smith."

Actually, Ruth had already acquired some experience, not

only with candidates but with Presidents. Once when Calvin Coolidge went to a ball game, the Yankees were lined up for formal introductions.

"How do you do, Mr. President," said Hoyt.

"Good day, sir," said Pennock.

Coolidge was walking slowly, shaking hands with each of the players, and Ruth, as he waited, took off his cap and wiped his forehead with a handkerchief.

"Mr. Ruth," President Coolidge said.

"Hot as hell, ain't it, Prez?" Mr. Ruth said.

People were always trying to reform him. Miller Huggins tried, first gently, then severely and ultimately with a $5,000 fine for breaking training. Ruth responded by holding Huggins at arm's length off the rear car of a speeding train. Christy Walsh, Ruth's agent and one of his many ghost writers, ultimately did convince Ruth that the $80,000 income would not long endure. Trust funds set up by Walsh and an attorney helped Ruth live out his years in comfort. Mrs. Claire Ruth succeeded somewhat in slowing her husband's pace, but significantly, at the end of his active baseball career, it was the old wild instinct that betrayed him.

After the 1934 season, in which Ruth's salary had dropped to $35,000, he realized that he was no longer a full-time player. Ruppert released him, and Ruth joined the Boston Braves as part-time outfielder and full-time vice president and assistant manager. The last two titles were meaningless. Judge Emil Fuchs, who owned the Braves, wanted Ruth to hit home runs. When Ruth failed—he was batting .181 in June—Fuchs dropped him as a ball player. The other two jobs promptly disappeared.

The specific was a party in New York. "I'm slumping," Ruth told Fuchs, "and a slumping ball player ought to get the hell away from the ball park. I want some time off." The French liner *Normandie,* then the largest ship afloat, was docking in New York, and Ruth had been invited to a welcoming brawl.

"Stay with the team," Fuchs ordered.

"I'm going to the party," Ruth said.

When Ruth went, Fuchs announced that team morale had been impaired and that Ruth, clearly, was neither managerial nor executive material.

The later years were not bright. Ruth wanted to manage in the majors, and the Yankees offered him their farm team in Newark, New Jersey. "You can't take care of yourself," Ruppert said. "How can I be sure you can take care of my best players? Newark, Ruth, or nothing."

"Nothing," Ruth said.

In 1938, Larry MacPhail hired him as a Dodger coach in midseason. That winter Leo Durocher, whose only talent in Ruth's view was a quick tongue, was appointed Brooklyn manager. Ruth resigned and was out of baseball for all time.

He lived in a large apartment on Riverside Drive, high above the Hudson River, and each year he threw a big birthday party for himself. He occupied his days with golf, fishing and watching baseball. Once he spoke at the Baseball Writers' dinner in New York. "I gave twenty-two years of my life to big league baseball," he said, "and I'm ready to give twenty-five more." Nearly a thousand baseball men heard him. No one offered him a job.

Was it simply Ruth's intemperance that kept him out of baseball? Or was it the mass resentment of club owners against a man whose personal impact pushed baseball salaries up as his own income soared? The reason is less important than the fact. Baseball turned away from the man who, more than anyone else, made it big business.

Yet till the end, outside the game, Ruth the man and Ruth the legend grew. Anywhere he wandered he was The Babe, unique, unrivaled, unchallenged. What made him happy was that children knew him. He loved children genuinely, as well might a man who had no childhood of his own. Nor any sons.

Cancer struck him in 1946, and he faced death, for two agonizing years, with utter disbelief. Dugan saw him when Ruth was confined to a wheelchair. "Joe," Ruth said, his voice cut to a whisper by the cancer. "Joe," he said, caught in the final horror of truth. "I'm gone, Joe. I'm gone." Dugan clutched his old friend's hand, and the two men wept. A few days later Ruth was dead.

"To understand him," says Dugan, who probably knew "Jidge" better than any man alive, "you had to understand this: He wasn't human. He was an animal. No human could have done the things he did and lived the way he did and been a ball player. Cobb? Could he pitch? Speaker? The rest? I saw them. I was there. There was never anybody close. When you figure the things he did and the way he lived and the way he played, you got to figure he was more than animal even. There never was anyone like him. He was a god."

Let the memory ring true, down to the last home run, down to the last bacchanal, through a small corridor of time.

The Day
Bobby Thomson Hit
His Home Run

Some days—they come rarely—are charged with public events so unexpected, so shocking, so far beyond the limits of belief, that the events are not really public at all. Their impact thrusts them into the private lives of millions of people, who forever after remember these events in personal terms.

Pearl Harbor day was like that. ("I was listening to the radio, a football game, when I heard about the bombing.") There was the day President Roosevelt died. ("I was riding the subway and the conductor told me. He was crying.") And then there was the day, in the most exciting of all baseball seasons, when Bobby Thomson hit his home run. . . .

The night before, nearly everyone slept well. Bobby Thomson was troubled because he had struck out with the bases full, but after a steak dinner and a few beers, he relaxed. Ralph Branca fell asleep quickly. He had pitched on Sunday, the last day of the regular season, and on Monday in the first game of the play-off. Tomorrow, October 3, 1951, would be Wednesday, and Branca did not expect that he would have to pitch again so soon.

Sal Maglie, who knew he was to start for the New York Giants, spent a comfortable night in his room at the Concourse Plaza Hotel. For all his intensity, Maglie had learned to control his nerves. So, to a degree, had Don Newcombe, who would start for the Brooklyn Dodgers. "I can always sleep," Newcombe said, a little proudly. "I don't need to take pills like some guys do the night before they pitch."

Charlie Dressen, who managed the Dodgers, went to an Italian restaurant, called Rocco's, and ate a dinner of clams, mussels, lobster and spaghetti with hot sauce. A few people asked how he felt about tomorrow's game, and Dressen told them he wasn't worried. "Our ball club is ready," he said.

One man who did feel restless was Andy Pafko, the new left fielder. The Dodgers had traded for Pafko at midseason, in a move the newspapers called pennant insurance, and Pafko, reading the papers, was impressed. Now he felt that the pennant was his personal responsibility. Lying in his room at the Hotel St. George in Brooklyn, he thought of his wife, Ellen, in Chicago. He had sent her a Pullman ticket to New York so she could watch him play with the Dodgers in the World Series. Next year there would be time to find an apartment together in Brooklyn, but for the moment Andy Pafko was alone. Perhaps it was loneliness as much as pressure that depressed him.

Although New York City was bright with the quickening pace of autumn, none of the ball players went out on the town. Everywhere, harboring their energies, they went to bed at about eleven o'clock, and soon, everywhere, they slept.

These were two tough and gifted baseball teams. The Dodgers had been built around such sluggers as Duke Snider and Gil Hodges, and in Jackie Robinson they had the finest competitor in baseball. For months that year the Dodgers won big and won often. On the night of August 11 they had been in first place, a full thirteen games ahead of the Giants, who were their closest competitors.

Under Leo Durocher the Giants were combative, strong in pitching and opportunism, concentrated in themselves. Bobby Thomson, like the other Giants, knew none of the Dodgers socially; the teams did not fraternize. He thought that Gil Hodges was a pleasant man but that the rest of the Dodgers were unpleasant. This was a sermon Durocher had preached ceaselessly throughout the last months of the season until finally the ball players came unquestioningly to believe their manager.

Durocher's Giants, jelling slowly, spent some of May in last place. It was only when Willie Mays was summoned from Minneapolis and Thomson became the regular third baseman that the team began to show fire. Then, from August 11 on, the Giants blazed, winning thirty-seven games and losing only seven under demanding, unrelenting pressure.

The Dodgers, playing .500 ball as some sluggers slumped, nonetheless seemed uncatchable by all the traditions of baseball. But the Giants, establishing new tradition, caught the uncatchable, forced them into a play-off and won the first game 3–1, defeating Ralph Branca at Ebbets Field. Then Clem Labine shut out the Giants at the Polo Grounds. The score was 10–0, but the game was close for some time and seemed to turn when Thomson, with bases full, struck out on a 3-and-2 pitch, a jumping curve that hooked wide of the plate.

No one expected the deciding game of the play-off to be easy, but no one, not Thomson, or Branca, or Durocher, or Dressen, felt any dramatic foreshadowing of what was ahead. The game would be tense, but they'd all been tense lately. It was against this background of tension, which the players accepted as a part of life, that everyone slept the night before.

Robert Brown Thomson, tall, swift and brown-haired, said good-bye to his mother at 9:50 A.M. and drove his blue Mercury to the Staten Island Ferry. The Thomsons lived on Flagg Place in New Dorp, once an independent village, now a community within the borough of Richmond. As he drove, Thomson thought about the game. "If I can just get three for four," he mused, then the old Jints will be all right." The thought comforted him. He'd been hitting well, and three for four seemed a reasonable goal.

Ralph Theodore Branca, tall, heavy-limbed and black-haired,

said good-bye to his mother at ten in suburban Mount Vernon, New York, the town where he had grown up, and drove off in his new Oldsmobile. He felt a little stiff from all his recent pitching. It would take him a long time to warm up, should Dressen need him in relief.

It was a gray day, darkened with the threat of rain. The temperature was warm enough—in the high 60s—but the crowd, waiting for the gates of the Polo Grounds bleachers to open, was smaller than the one which had waited in bright sunshine the day before.

Most of the players arrived by car. Andy Pafko came by subway, an hour's ride from downtown Brooklyn. "I'll beat the crowd," he decided, "so there's no sense wasting money on a cab." The crowd, it was to develop, was scarcely worth beating: 34,320, some 15,000 under standing-room capacity.

Shaped like a football horseshoe, the Polo Grounds made strange demands on pitchers. The foul line in right field ran only 250 feet until it reached the lower deck of the grandstands. The left-field line ran slightly longer, but in left a scoreboard was fixed to the façade of the upper deck, a façade that extended several yards closer to the plate than did the lower stands. A short fly, drifting down toward a fielder, became a home run merely by grazing that projecting scoreboard.

Both walls fell away sharply, and the fence in center field was 485 feet distant. The pitching rule, then, was to make the batter hit to center, where distance didn't matter. The outfielding rule was to crowd the middle. The right and left fielders conceded drives down the line and tried to prevent hits from carrying into the deep alleys in left and right center. At the Polo Grounds, outfielders stood in a tightly bunched row, all seemingly about the same distance from home plate.

Back of center field stood a squat green building that looked like an outsized pillbox and contained the clubhouses, a dining room for the press and an apartment for Horace Stoneham, the Giants' owner. Since both Durocher and Dressen believed in intensive managing, each team was gathered for a meeting in that green building shortly before noon. The announced purpose was to review hitters, although the two teams had played each other twenty-four times previously that season and there was nothing fresh or new to say about anyone.

"Jam Mueller on the fists," Dressen told Don Newcombe. "Keep the ball low and away to Thomson. Don't let him pull it." Dressen concluded, with more warmth than he customarily displayed: "Look, I know it's tough to have to play this game, but remember we did our best all year. So today, let's just go out and do the best we can."

"Don't give Hodges anything inside," Durocher told Maglie. Then, later: "We haven't quit all year. We won't quit now. Let's go get 'em."

During batting practice Branca was standing near the cage with Pee Wee Reese and Jackie Robinson. "You guys get butterflies?" a reporter asked.

"No matter how long you been playing, you still get butterflies before the big ones," Reese said. Robinson grinned, and Branca nodded solemnly. Ralph's long face, in repose, was sad or, perhaps, deadpan. One never knew whether he felt troubled by what was around him or whether he was about to laugh.

The game began badly for the Giants. Sal Maglie, who had won twenty-three games and beaten the Dodgers five times that season, walked Reese and Duke Snider in the first inning. Jackie Robinson came up and lined Maglie's first pitch safely into left field for a single. Reese scored, and the Dodgers were ahead 1–0.

Newcombe was fast but not untouchable, and in the second inning Lockman reached him for a single. Thomson followed with a sharp drive to left, his first hit, and briefly the Giants seemed to be rallying. But very briefly. Running with his head down, Thomson charged past first base and had almost reached second before he noticed that Lockman had stopped there. Thomson was tagged out in a rundown, an embarrassing end to the threat.

When the day grew darker and the lights were turned on as

the third inning began, the ball park buzzed with countless versions of a joke: "Well, now maybe Thomson will be able to see what he's doing."

During the fifth Thomson doubled, his second hit, and Branca began to throw. Newcombe pitched out of the inning easily, but Branca threw a little longer. He wasn't snapping curves or firing fast balls. He was just working to loosen his arm, shoulder and back.

Branca threw again during the sixth inning, and when Monte Irvin doubled to left in the seventh, Branca began to throw hard. He felt loose by then. His fast ball was alive. Carl Erskine, warming up next to him, was bouncing his curve, but Branca had good control and good stuff.

With Irvin at second, Lockman pushed a bunt in front of the plate, and Rube Walker, the Dodger catcher, grabbed the ball and threw to Billy Cox at third. Irvin beat the throw, and now Thomson came to bat with the tying run at third base late in a 1–0 ball game.

Bearing down, Newcombe threw only strikes. After two, Thomson fouled off a fast ball. Then he hit another fast ball deep into center field, and Irvin scored easily after the catch. As the eighth inning began, the score was 1–1.

"I got nothing left, nothing," Newcombe announced as he walked into the Dodger dugout. Jackie Robinson and Roy Campanella, who was not playing that day because he had pulled a thigh muscle, took Newcombe aside.

"My arm's tight," Newcombe said.

"Bullshit," Robinson said. "You go out there and pitch until your goddamned arm falls off."

"Roomie," Campanella said, "you ain't gonna quit on us now. You gonna hum that pea for us, roomie."

While the two built a fire under Newcombe, other Dodgers were making the inning miserable for both Maglie and Thomson. Reese and Snider opened with singles to right, and when Maglie threw a curve in the dirt and past Wes Westrum, Reese scored and Snider sped to third. Then Maglie walked Robinson, and the Dodgers, ahead 2–1, once again had runners at first and third.

Pafko pulled a bounding ball up the third-base line and Thomson, breaking nicely, reached backhand for it. The play required a delicate touch; the ball glanced off the heel of Thomson's glove and skidded away from him. Snider scored, making it 3–1 Brooklyn, and Pafko was credited with a single. Then Billy Cox followed with a fierce one-hopper, again to Thomson's sector.

One thought—"Get in front of it"—crossed Thomson's mind. He did, lunging recklessly. There were other times at third when Thomson had thought of hard smashes coming up and hitting him in the face. This time he didn't. He thought only of blocking the ball with his glove, his arm, his chest. But the ball bounced high and carried over his shoulder into left field. The Dodgers had their third run of the inning and a 4–1 lead.

Newcombe blazed through the eighth, his arm no longer tight, and Larry Jansen retired the Dodgers in the ninth. "Come on," Durocher shouted as the last of the ninth began. "We can still get 'em. Come on."

Newcombe threw two quick strikes to Alvin Dark. "Got to get my bat on the ball," Dark thought. "Just get my bat on it."

Newcombe threw again, and Dark rapped a bounder into the hole in the right side of the infield. Both Hodges and Robinson broke for the ball and Newcombe ran to cover first base. Hodges, straining, touched the ball with the tip of his mitt and deflected it away from Robinson. Perhaps if he had not touched it, Robinson could have made the play. As it was, Dark reached first. A single, ruled the scorer.

It was then that Dressen made a curious decision. He let Hodges hold the bag on Dark, as though Dark as a base runner were important. Actually, of course, Dark could have stolen second, third and home without affecting the game. The Giants needed three runs to tie, not one, and the Dodgers needed only outs.

A fine point, except that Don Mueller, up next, bounced a

single through the right side—close to Hodges' normal fielding depth. Now the Giants had runners at first and third. All around the Polo Grounds people stood up in excitement.

With Monte Irvin coming to bat, Dressen walked to the mound. Branca and Erskine were throwing in the bullpen, and Clyde Sukeforth, the bullpen coach, had told Dressen that Branca was fast and loose. But on the way to the mound the Dodger manager thought about catching, not pitching.

Campanella had a way with Newcombe. He knew how to needle the big pitcher to fury, and this fury added speed to Newcombe's fast ball. Walking to the mound, Dressen wondered about replacing Rube Walker with Campanella. There was only one drawback. Foul territory at the Polo Grounds was extensive. A rodeo, billed as colossal, was once staged entirely in the foul area there. Campanella, with his bad leg, could catch, but he could not run after foul pops. Dressen thought of Hodges and Cox, both sure-handed, both agile. They could cover for Campanella to some extent. But there was all that area directly behind home plate where no one would be able to help Campy at all. Dressen thought of a foul pop landing safely on the sod directly below the press box. He thought of the newspapers the next day. The second-guessing would be fierce. He didn't want that. No, Dressen decided, it wouldn't be worth that. He chatted with Newcombe for a moment and went back to the dugout. When Irvin fouled out to Hodges, Dressen decided that he had done the right thing.

Then Newcombe threw an outside fast ball to Whitey Lockman, and Lockman doubled to left. Dark scored, making it 4–2, but Mueller, in easily at third, slid badly and twisted his ankle. He could neither rise nor walk. Clint Hartung ran for him, and action suspended while Mueller was carried to the distant Giant clubhouse.

"Branca's ready," Clyde Sukeforth told Charlie Dressen on the intercom that ran from dugout to bullpen.

"Okay," Dressen said. "I want him."

Branca felt strong and loose as he started his long walk in from the bullpen. At that moment he had only one thought. Thomson was the next batter, and he wanted to get ahead of Thomson. Branca never pitched in rigid patterns. He adjusted himself to changing situations, and his thought now was simply to get his first pitch over the plate with something on it.

Coming into the infield, he remembered the pregame conversation with the newspaperman. "Any butterflies?" he said to Robinson and Reese. They grinned, but not very widely.

At the mound, Dressen handed Branca the ball and said: "Get him out." Without another word the manager turned and walked back to the dugout.

Watching Branca take his eight warm-up pitches, Thomson thought of his own goal. He had two hits. Another now would give him his three for four. It would also tie the score.

"Boy," Durocher said to Thomson, "if you ever hit one, hit one now." Thomson nodded but said nothing. Then he stepped up to the plate.

Branca's first pitch was a fast ball, hip-high over the inside corner. "Should have swung at that," Thomson told himself, backing out of the box.

"I got my strike," thought Branca. Now it was time to come up and in with a fast ball. Now it was time for a bad pitch that might tempt Thomson to waste a swing. If he went for the bad ball, chances were he'd miss. If he took it, Branca would still be ready to come back with a curve, low and away. Branca was moving the ball around, a basic point when pitching to good hitters.

The pitch came in high and tight, just where Branca had wanted it. Thomson swung hard and the ball sailed out toward left.

"Get down, get down," screamed Billy Cox as the line drive carried high over his head.

"I got a chance at it," thought Andy Pafko, bolting back toward the fence.

Then the ball was gone, under the overhanging scoreboard, over the high wall, gone deep into the seats in lower left, 320 feet from home plate. For seconds, which seemed like minutes, the crowd sat dumb. Then came the roar. It was a roar matched all across the country, wherever people sat at radio or television sets, a roar of delight, a roar of horror, but mostly a roar of utter shock. It was a moment when all the country roared and when an office worker in a tall building on Wall Street, hearing a cry rise all about her, wondered if war had been declared.

As the ball sailed into the stands, Thomson danced around the bases, skipping and leaping. The Giants crowded from their dugout to home plate. Ed Stanky, the second baseman, ran to Durocher, jumped on the manager's back, wrestled him to the ground and embraced him.

In left, Pafko stood stunned. Then he started to walk slowly toward the clubhouse, telling himself over and over: "It can't be." Most of the Dodgers were walking before Thomson reached second base. Jackie Robinson held his ground. He wanted to make sure that Thomson touched all bases before conceding that the Giants had won, 5–4, before conceding that the pennant race was over.

Clyde Sukeforth gathered gear in the bullpen, and nearby Carl Erskine turned to Clem Labine. "That's the first time I've seen a big fat wallet go flying into the seats," Erskine said.

As Thomson touched home plate, the Giants lifted him to their shoulders. Then, inexplicably, they lowered him, and everyone ran for the clubhouse. Champagne was waiting. "Gee whizz," Thomson said. "Gee whizz."

Wes Westrum and Clint Hartung grabbed Ed Stanky, who liked to boast that he had never been drunk, and pinned him to a rubbing table. Westrum poured champagne into Stanky's mouth. "You're gonna get drunk now," he shouted. Westrum turned to the rubbing table, where Mueller lay, ice packs at his ankle. "Hey, Don," he shouted and emptied a magnum over the injured leg.

"Isn't this the damnedest thing you ever saw?" Durocher said.

"Gee whizz," Thomson said. "Gee whizz."

"How the hell did you go into second with Lockman there?" Coach Fred Fitzsimmons said to Thomson. "But the hell with that," he added, and kissed Thomson damply.

"Congratulations," Charlie Dressen said to Durocher. "I told you we'd finish one-two. Well, we did, and I'm number two."

"Gee whizz," Thomson said.

In the Dodger dressing room, Branca wept, showered slowly and, after submitting to some questioning, asked reporters to leave him alone. Then he went to the Oldsmobile, where his fiancée, blonde Ann Mulvey, was waiting with Father Frank Rowley of Fordham.

"Why me?" Branca said inside the car. "I don't smoke. I don't drink. I don't run around. Baseball is my whole life. Why me?"

"God chose you," the priest said, "because He knew you had faith and strength enough to bear this cross."

Branca nodded and felt a little better.

Thomson went from the ball park to a CBS studio where he appeared on Perry Como's regular Wednesday night television show. Everywhere he went he was cheered, and always three thoughts ran through his mind. The old Jints had won. He had pushed his runs-batted-in total up over one hundred. He had got his three for four.

When Thomson reached the house in New Dorp, his older brother, Jim, was waiting for him. "Do you know what you've done?" Jim said, all intensity and earnestness.

Only then, six hours after the event, did Bobby Thomson realize that his home run was something that other people would remember for all the rest of his days.

They Ain't Getting
No Maiden

Cornered by acquaintances, Leo Ernest Durocher of West Springfield, Massachusetts, Brooklyn, Manhattan, Chicago, Houston and Beverly Hills, concedes that his life story would make a superior movie. It possesses heroic, even epic qualities, Leo suggests without coyness. "And besides, my buddy Sinatra wants to play me."

That, I suspect, is rather a hustle. Whether Leo operates at cards, at baseball, at life, a hustle is built in. With time a man does best to cease moralizing and stand back in admiration of all that gall and glitter. ("You got the cash? Good. Turns out Frank's tied up with his retirement, but there's another guy who's ready and he can act a ton. Vic Damone.")

I was hustled cleanly by Leo aeons ago when he was prodding the press to criticize the New York Giants, following weeks of soporific play. "Charlie Zorch," Leo was saying, using the real name of a Giant regular, "is the dumbest, laziest s.o.b. I ever managed. I want you to know that and you can even print it. Except don't use my name." Zapped in the press, Zorch could reasonably be expected to protest. Leo would then respond: "That writer is the dumbest, laziest s.o.b. I ever met. You got to show him up for all of us." Raging, inspired, Zorch might wallop two home runs. At least that was the script Durocher imagined. A victory won at imperceptible cost: the bruised pride of a writer who lacked Leo's overview of the uses of the press.

After listening to Durocher criticize Giant ball players one afternoon, I hubristically quoted him by name. He withdrew all quotes, stopped speaking to me and made a number of phone calls. Subsequently the management of the New York *Herald Tribune* instructed me to apologize to Durocher or forfeit my $10,000-a-year job. Righteous as Cromwell, I resigned.

No matter. Ten years later I understood, as Leo does, that $200 a week doesn't carry a man far first-class, and Leo, now introducing himself as chum, was asking my counsel, while he hustled the dying *Saturday Evening Post* out of $50,000 for a short-form, nonfilmic version of his life.

"These guys want everything for a lousy fifty Gs," he complained.

"Everything," I said, "is what they're paying you the fifty for."

"But I gotta save some stuff. I promised Frank."

Such attitudes have won Leo a simmering press. Sportswriters point out that he is moody, contentious, suspicious, egocentric, "but aside from that one hell of a man." Indeed, a parable attributed to Dick Young of the New York *Daily News* goes further. "You and Durocher are on a raft," Young suggests. "A wave comes and knocks him into the ocean. You dive in and save his life. A shark comes and takes your leg. Next day, you and Leo start out even."

As sometimes happens, the working press has been overwhelmed by specifics. Certainly Leo is moody, contentious, etc. He is no man's ideal mate on Kon-Tiki. But it is a mark of a certain purity of spirit that he has passed the age of Social Security eligibility largely as he was twenty-five years before. Leo manipulates. Leo mistrusts. Leo uses. Leo abuses. But his salient, enduring quality is a lovely rage.

In the old Brooklyn Dodger clubhouse, a telephone once was

fastened to a wall. On a day when the team lost by a close score, the late Gil Hodges answered a call from his wife. Durocher listened with wild surmise as Hodges repeated his instructions: five pounds of potatoes; leaf spinach; two quarts milk. When you're a big league ball player, Leo believes, there's only one way to take a loss. Lose hard. Don't, damnit, lose and be an errand boy for the old lady. No, damnit. That's wrong. After Hodges hung up, Durocher ripped the telephone loose and slammed it to the concrete floor. Even after he had been dismissed as Dodger manager, the telephone was not replaced.

When Durocher went to work in Houston during 1972, his reputation showed flakes at the edges. During the five previous seasons in Chicago, he had not won a pennant for the Cubs. True, he converted a losing ball club into a contender, and Chicago attendance doubled during his stay. But in Durocher's phrase, "I come to win." He came to Chicago and never finished better than second. Polite decorum toward his newest employers seemed in order for a recently fired manager within waving distance of his seventieth birthday.

At the Astrodome a telephone line ran from the owners' private box into the dugout, and the owners liked to offer commentary on the way a manager ran the team. Durocher arrived, pronounced the Houston Astros full of promise, smiled at a huddle of Texas journalists and went to work. On his third night the dugout telephone rang. Something about a change of pitchers. Durocher had been concentrating on the ball game, and the phone call threatened his concentration. With his strong shortstop's hands, Leo ripped this telephone from the dugout wall. His integrity survived. Management stopped nagging him. AT&T stock was doing passably again within six months.

The time to watch him, perhaps the best time, was when he hit Chicago after a decade on the beach. Earning a living, to be sure. Turning a profit some years. But not working at his special craft. As that season, 1967, entered its hard, hot summer, Durocher was approaching his sixty-second birthday head on. He had just confided to an interviewer that he was fifty-nine years old, although earlier he had confided to the *Official Encyclopedia of Baseball,* revised edition, that he was born on July 27, 1905. He had outworn his welcome in many towns, and he was fifty-nine going on sixty-two. By any standard that was an unsettling situation.

What cheered the man and nourished his ego was that he again found himself working at what he believed The Guy Upstairs—his favorite term for The Divinity—intended him to do. After ten years of other employment, Durocher was managing in the major leagues. The Chicago Cubs, the team Durocher led, may have been the worst of twenty. Their organization was sterile, their owner, P. K. Wrigley *(Hi, ho, hey, hey,/Chew your little troubles away),* was remote and the team broke last that season. But he was happy in his new job, Durocher insisted. "As long as I can walk out there," he said, "managing is what I want to do."

There was no question that Durocher wanted the Cub job. A larger question was how long would he continue to want it. No fewer than nine of Durocher's former players were managing in the major leagues, and the four in the National League would beat his brains out more often than not. That burned a man, particularly after he had built his career on total victory, particularly after he had bought himself the highest house in the most expensive subdivision in America, particularly when he was fifty-nine going on sixty-two and impatient.

A few years earlier, when he was married to Laraine Day, the Mormon actress, Durocher believed The Guy Upstairs had larger plans for him, including capital gains. The Cleveland Indians asked him to manage for a $35,000 salary plus $10,000 expenses, plus a lucrative, complex stock deal. "Better up the stock deal a little," said Durocher, the capital-gainsman. When the Indians did not, he was disappointed and at liberty.

Yet he was offended when Charles O. Finley subsequently

offered him a job managing Kansas City in the American League. "I'll pay you fifty thousand on a two- or three-year contract to come to Kansas City," said Finley, misjudging his man.

"Mr. Finley," said Leo, at ease in Beverly Hills, "if I want a steak, I'll send for it."

So, with some second thoughts on overconfidence, Durocher found himself working from 1961 through 1964 as a coach under Walter Alston, manager of the Los Angeles Dodgers and a stolid bucolic. One thing Durocher knew about The Guy Upstairs. He did not intend Leo to end up as a coach under a farmer. But, Leo reasoned, Alston might get fired and he might be hired as the successor. Tension between Alston and Durocher did not all by itself cause the Dodgers to blow the 1962 pennant, but the club was sharply divided between Durocher men and Alston men. It didn't win.

After a rousing comeback in 1963, the team collapsed to sixth and the Dodger front office concluded that someone had to go. Leo was dismissed, and Alston was retained. To make sure Durocher could not charge persecution, the Dodgers fired all their other coaches, too, including Joe Becker, a friend of Alston's, and a man Alston very much wanted to keep.

While these maneuverings were transpiring in Los Angeles, the Cubs in another part of the forest offered comic relief. No one was plotting to manage the Cubs because, among other reasons, the Cubs didn't have a manager. Instead, P. K. Wrigley instituted a College of Coaches, a sort of brain trust of half a dozen men who took turns running the team.

In 1966, with Durocher employed as a discless jockey answering questions and orating for ninety minutes a night on radio station KABC in L.A., Wrigley reached a decision. Checking his attendance figures—about 640,000, or roughly a million under what Bill Veeck had once drawn with the Chicago White Sox —he recoiled as though stung, then said, "John, find me a talented and experienced man."

John Holland, a fifty-six-year-old Oklahoma conservative who was vice president of the Cubs, said, "Well, Durocher is both."

Within weeks the Chicago Cubs joyously announced the engagement of Leo Durocher. "But we have no immediate announcement as to Durocher's title," an official said. "We have found from long experience that it doesn't make any difference what title a team leader has as long as he has the ability to take charge."

Durocher considered the remark and the Cubs' long experience. "I just gave myself a title," he said. "I'm not the head coach here. I'm the manager."

He was indeed. He is one of the very best of baseball managers. In sixteen seasons with the Brooklyn Dodgers and the New York Giants, Durocher teams won three pennants, one World Series and had an overall percentage of .560. True, teams managed by Casey Stengel won three times as many pennants, and teams managed by Al Lopez had a better winning percentage, .588. But in baseball, numbers seldom provide a full measure of a man.

The special genius of Durocher is not only in the victory but in the manner. He is, all by himself and at once, innovator, symbol and creator. Those nine managers who once played for him view him variously with idolatry, admiration and dislike. None has ignored him or his influence.

"My kind of team" Durocher says of clubs he built at Brooklyn and New York, and baseball men perceive a combative image. Both times he started with uncertain material, although better than what he had at Chicago, and produced arrogant and exciting champions.

He makes phrases, strong, memorable ones, although lately it has pleased his fancy to protest that he never actually said, or anyway didn't actually mean, the one that may yet get him into Bartlett: "Nice guys finish last." Mostly he fights. Mostly, if his interest does not flag, he'll stay up late nights and get up early mornings to win. He'll bellow, beg, intimidate, curse, bless, to win. He'll kick and scratch and brawl and charm to win, and these are some of the things Durocher says:

"I'd bench my brother. I come to kill ya. Anybody can finish second, but I got to win. If we're spittin' at a goddamn crack in the wall for pennies, I got to beat ya. Maybe I don't understand that word 'sportsmanship,' but this is professional. What are we out at the park for except to win? I'd trip my mother. I'll help her up, brush her off, tell her I'm sorry. *But Mother don't make it to third.*"

To an extent Durocher is a prisoner of his glibness. With the essentially docile Cubs he had to labor for viciousness, seeking out words and phrases that proved he was just as mean as ever, as though the discovery of some ball-field kindness would undo it all, the revelation that he suffered bouts of civility and compassion would end the dream and transform him suddenly into something pallid, a ghost of Leo the Great.

At the start, he could not be rough with the players. They had no confidence any more. Nor did he feel he could be rough with his employers. Thirty-seven years before, arguing about his salary, he cursed an employer, the general manager of the Yankees. He never was allowed to play for the Yankees again. That left, as an outlet for hostility and a proving ground that he had not gone soft, the sportswriters who covered the team. Durocher did not win many games for the Cubs in April and early May, but he cursed more sportswriters than any manager in either league.

The rules, he explained to the press, were simple but absolute. "I don't answer none of your double-barreled questions," Durocher said. "If you're wondering what a double-barreled question is, it's one you can't answer right either way, like how long you been beating your wife. Now, boys, there's no sense in asking me those questions because I'm not going to answer them, and anybody who says I will or ever did is a liar."

A New York newspaperman, who wanted to interview him on opening day in San Francisco, approached softly as Durocher slouched in the front seat of the team bus.

"Nah," said Durocher. "I ain't giving any goddamn interviews. I got enough goddamn troubles now."

He had a cold. Well, he didn't know whether it was a cold or a virus or what, but when the Cubs got to L.A., he was going to see his doc and get fixed up. "Damn," he said. "I don't know what it is."

He might still have been the Giants' manager if he had not outworn his welcome with them, too, and it was a hard thing for him at Candlestick Park, looking out at the two teams, his and theirs. The Cubs had a fine third baseman in Ron Santo and a good outfielder in Billy Williams. Both hit with power. But the club professional, Ernie Banks, seemed suddenly old when he swung. The other talent stumbled a long way from competence.

"You had one of those great springs," Durocher said on the field at Candlestick to Willie Mays. He had brought Mays into the majors, reared him, so to speak, and here was Willie playing for the other club. The other club had all the talent, even his own.

"Not too bad, Leo. Not too bad," Willie said.

"You hit .383 with nine home runs," Durocher said.

"I didn't see no figures," Mays said.

"Willie," Leo said, "this is me you're talking to. Me. I know ya, Willie. You got the figures written on the inside of your shoes."

It was an unpleasant afternoon for Durocher. In the fourth inning Mays hit a home run, and the Giants scored six times. Later, after Len Gabrielson hit another homer, a Chicago pitcher named Bill Faul threw two pitches at Mays' head.

Willie took three steps toward Faul and shouted something. That was all. The Giants won, as the wind came hooting up the bay, by 9 to 1.

Afterward, a portly, elderly baseball writer said to Durocher in the clubhouse, "I guess when you were quoted telling Willie to stay loose at the plate you meant it, eh, Leo?"

Durocher still felt weak from the virus, or whatever it was.

He couldn't get warm, he said. The press felt sorry for this new old manager who had lost big on opening day.

"Quoted where?" Durocher said, clearing hoarseness from his throat as his voice rose.

"In a spring-training story," the baseball writer said.

"You're not asking the right question," Durocher said. "Why don't you ask me if I said it?" He called the writer by name, schoolteacherly. Then he shouted, "Why don't you ask me if I said it?" Suddenly Durocher did not feel weak any longer. "Because if you ask me if I said it, I'm going to tell you I didn't. Never. Never did. And any man who says I did is a liar. You are a goddamn liar, friend."

Opening day in Chicago was no better. Already the Cubs were 1 and 5, and now they had to play against the Giants again. On the way to Wrigley Field, Durocher turned into Lake Shore Drive on a changing light, and a car plowed into the back of his Buick Riviera. He was not hurt, but he had to ride the rest of the way in a squad car. That bothered him, and so had a forthright series of articles in the Chicago *Daily News* called "Durocher: The Legend and the Man." It was a wet day and chilly, and the stands were not full, but on the field Durocher found himself surrounded by interviewers. For a little while he was cordial, saying orthodox things. "I don't see how this club didn't finish higher with all the talent it's got. We're gonna cause a little trouble. Make a little noise."

After a while he was talking into a microphone held by Rudy Bukich, then quarterback of the Chicago Bears, and when that was through it was time to attack again. "Ya gettin' this all down?" he barked at a newspaperman. "Yeah, yeah. The writers come around and they're real nice, like that guy from the *Daily News*. He was sitting by the pool, and I couldn't have been nicer, and all the while ya know what he had up his sleeve? A goddamn hatchet. Well, yah, you can all get your hatchets out, boys, and work on me all you want, cause I got news for you boys, it's been done before. When they hatchet me, they ain't getting no goddamn maiden."

The style is first to try intimidation. After that, perhaps amiability. "Now there is no sense," Durocher says, "if you are going for a pennant, of being mean to a bad club. If I'm on the contender and we're playing the last-place team, it's how do ya do. Glad to see ya. Welcome to town. Take 'em out. Buy 'em a drink. Beat 'em a run or two. That's fine. Don't show 'em up. They're sleeping dogs, kid, and you know what they say about them." The style is always loud, but flexible.

He is an absolute pragmatist in all things. "With a girl, you've got to make your move fast," Durocher once instructed a younger man. "Say you pick her up at seven o'clock. Well, then grab her where it tickles at 7:05. No go? Tough, but hell it's early yet. There's still time to call another broad. But say that move you make at 7:05 works. She says okay. Well, then, hello my dear. You'd be surprised. Some damned famous broads say okay quick."

Durocher came out of West Springfield, Massachusetts, schooled in poolrooms and streets, with a blurred background. There have been reports in the past that he is part Jewish. Durocher says no, that is not so. The name is French. His antecedents are French-Canadian. He seldom talks about his father. Once he told a biographer that he had spent his life looking for father images.

He was an expedient ball player rather than gifted. He had good hands, quickness, drive and profound self-knowledge. He played shortstop, a good position for a weak hitter since defensive shortstops are at a premium. His throwing arm was not outstanding, but he taught himself to scoop and throw with remarkable speed. He is credited by baseball men with being the best of all shortstops at getting rid of the ball in a hurry.

He never could hit. His lifetime major league average of .247 was acquired in decades when batting averages were higher than they are now. Someone who played with him on the sandlots of West Springfield says that he could not hit even then. "I don't know what it was," Durocher once said. "The guy would pitch, and my butt would fly out. Good-bye." The reference is to a slight, significant, involuntary movement that carried his weight away from the speeding pitch. Excellent self-defense; poor batting form.

He appeared, incredibly, on what may have been the greatest of all hitting teams, the Yankees of Babe Ruth and Lou Gehrig. Up for a sip of Ruppert's beer in 1925, Durocher made the Yankees in 1928 and played in 102 games. Some of the older men called him "Fifth Avenue" because of his garish clothing, and he seems to have been nothing more than a boisterous spear carrier for two years. But there he was, the expedient ball player with a great Yankee team, until he told off his employer and had to play for Cincinnati, an exile that lasted four years.

He was always moving, wearing out a welcome, and at twenty-eight he was dealt to St. Louis, where he played shortstop for the Gashouse Gang, loudly and well. He came to Brooklyn in 1938, when the Cardinals tired of his noise after a season in which he batted .203. Larry MacPhail, a skilled and raucous promoter, had come into Brooklyn, and word was that Mac-Phail was looking for a new manager for 1939.

There were two prominent candidates for the job. One was Durocher, by now famous for his ferocious drive to win. The other was Babe Ruth, whom MacPhail had hired as a coach. Late in that lost season in Brooklyn long ago, a young baseball writer reported that Ruth, coaching at first, had flashed the hit-and-run sign to a batter.

Now that was a joke, Durocher said in the clubhouse at Ebbets Field. How could the big baboon have flashed a hit-and-run sign when he didn't even know what the sign was? Probably what Durocher said was true. Signs and inside baseball were alien to Ruth. But he had been publicly humiliated, and Ruth decided to avenge himself on Durocher with his fists. He made the threat while seated on a three-legged stool before a narrow locker.

Quickly Durocher shoved Babe Ruth into the locker and

cuffed him about the face. "I knew," Durocher said later, "that if the big guy got to me first, I'd be a goner. I also knew fights get broken up fast. By shoving him in there I figured I'd get my shots in, and before he could come back at me, the fight would be over."

Just before the season ended, Durocher was playing bridge on a train when Cookie Lavagetto made an inept play. "Damnit, ain'cha got any brains?" Durocher said.

Ruth had been reading a comic strip. Now he looked up. "Yeah, Bananas," Ruth said to Lavagetto. "Don't ya know that the only guy on this club with any brains is the big man?" And Babe Ruth solemnly pointed to the big man, Leo Durocher.

Durocher became manager in 1939, and the Dodgers jumped from seventh place to third. They won the pennant in 1941 and have been contenders more often than not ever since.

In mid-1948 he became the manager of the Giants, then a squad of strong, slow sluggers. "I'm gonna build my kind of team," Durocher promised. A swift, gifted, opportunistic Durocher Giant team won the pennant in 1951. Since then the Giants, too, have been contenders more often than not.

Durocher's Giant welcome wore out in 1955, one season after his club had won the World Series. With familiarity, he became inclined to make sarcastic remarks about the Giant management, telling a story here and another there among his friends. One friend, Danny Kaye, later entertained scores of people at a banquet with an imitation of a Giant executive. It was a crude, unbuttoned performance, but it made Durocher laugh out loud. When the laughter reached the highest offices of the Giants, it became one more of the complex of reasons that led the Giants to fire him.

After that Leo announced that he would never manage again unless he was given "a piece of the club." Sour years followed. He worked at NBC, but that job evaporated. He missed the chance at Cleveland. His marriage to Laraine Day ended, transporting him from a comfortable home to bachelor quarters. He was hard put to maintain his lavish standard and so, with much talk of swallowing pride and a great dumbshow of humility, he took a job in 1961 as coach under a farmer.

There were painful days for coach Durocher and manager Walter Alston. "We're in Cincinnati," Durocher says, recalling one day of frustration, "and they got a man on and Don Drysdale is pitching to Gordie Coleman, which is a low-ball pitcher pitching to a low-ball hitter, and the fellows on the bench, some of the players, said, 'What would you do, Leo?'

"I said, I'd put him on because Marty Keough, the hitter after Coleman, is a high-ball hitter. Well, Alston don't put him on, and the first ball pitched to Coleman, boom, a home run, and now we're down 3–0. But I'm not second-guessing Alston. I made this statement before Drysdale ever pitched the ball.

"All right. The eighth inning. We score a run. We tie in the ninth 3–3. In the tenth we score three, and now it's 6–3. Looks great. They're up. First man singles and the next man doubles. The tying run at the plate and nobody out.

"Alston finally tells me to bring in a relief pitcher, Ed Roebuck. The next man hits a fly ball, scoring a run, making it 6–4, and the man on second went to third. Next man hit another fly. It's 6–5. Two outs. Nobody on. Next man doubled. Coleman the batter.

"Now they ask me. I said, 'Why didn't you ask me earlier, that other time? You're asking me now.' And I said, 'Put him on.'

"They said, 'How can you put the winning run on?'

"I says, *'If you're scared, go home.'*

"So Alston got teed off, but finally they did what I said, put him on, and the first ball pitched to Keough, the next hitter, right back to the pitcher. Game's over. We're in the clubhouse."

Afterward Durocher and Alston were undressing in front of adjoining lockers, when a reporter asked Alston, "How come you put the winning run on?"

"Well, I thought about that," Alston said slowly. "It was a kinda tough decision, but I thought it was the right thing to do."

Durocher moved his gear and dressed a good distance from Alston after that. He will not talk about him any longer.

Durocher did not have to take the job with the Cubs, although he had gone deeply into debt building a mansion while he was a Dodger coach. The house, which cost perhaps $200,-000, is located in Trousdale Estates, a Beverly Hills development that advertises sites for $54,000 and up. But his radio program was lucrative. He landed some television jobs. According to a former agent, Durocher out of baseball in 1965 earned more than $75,000.

The real reason he took the Chicago job, Durocher said, was that he didn't see how the Cubs could "finish eighth with all those good ball players." For openers he went on the road in Illinois, through Peoria, Joliet and the rest, with some players and a spiel. "Now look at my club," he'd say. "Mr. Ellsworth, the left-hander. Who's a better one? Koufax? Right. Who else is better? Nobody. There's nobody. Mr. Williams in my outfield. One of the five best players in the game. Let me tell you, we got speed, legmen and some power and . . ."

He doubled the Cubs' advance sale. It is kindless to point out that Ellsworth lost his first four starts and that Williams was batting .215 on May 15. "Leo had those guys convinced back in January," says Joe Black, a former Dodger, who caught some of the road show. "They really thought they were good. Trouble is they didn't open the season till April. The spell wore off."

When he left Chicago, the Cubs' College of Coaches had been forgotten. Whitey Lockman, the old Giant first baseman, succeeded him, ironically the tenth Durocher player to become a major league manager. But more than at Brooklyn, or New York, there was a sense Durocher had failed. He hadn't won. That's what you heard. He hadn't won. And then the specifics again. Needless feuding with the press. Overmanaging his pitching staff. Poor communication with certain ball players. Bickering with sportscasters. *Hell, he hadn't won.*

Durocher went to Houston and hired a Spanish-speaking

coach to communicate with Latin ball players. He smiled cheerfully by way of charming the Texas press. He risked everything by ripping out that dugout telephone.

Years ago one would not have thought to call him admirable. It was as if all life were an enormous poolroom and everyone had to be hustled before he hustled you. But I wonder about that myself. Perhaps Leo is right: for real-estate salesmen and baseball managers and obstetricians and lawyers and authors, perhaps beyond a certain point the name of the game is hustle.

That is something to take under advisement. Meanwhile, cheers to a pragmatist, true to himself and defiant of time, after almost seven decades.

Willie's Song

He is sitting on the three-legged stool they give to ball players and milkmaids, and he looks enormous and supple and strong. He has a massive flat chest and bulging arms and shoulders and the kind of muscled stomach I remember from comic-book drawings of Tarzan. Still, he is thirty-eight years old.

"What do you do to stay in shape, Will?" I say.

"Nothin' special," Willie Mays says. "I walk a lot and I play golf now, 'stead of pool. And I don't eat too much and I never did drink, except three times when we won pennants." A smile briefly lights the handsome, mobile face.

"Well, you look as if you can go on forever."

"I won't lie to you," Mays says. "It gets to be work. Sometimes when I get tired and all that pressure, it gets to be work. I knew when I was sixteen years old, I never did want to work for a living." Again the smile.

"You want to manage?"

"Yeah. I think I'd like to."

"What about handling pitchers? Could you do that?"

"You're a manager," Willie says, "man, you get to hire help."

It is eleven o'clock the morning after a night game, and Willie will play this afternoon. His team, still the San Francisco Giants, is not going well, and last night in the ninth inning, with the count 3 and 2, he guessed curve. Then Ron Taylor of the Mets threw a fast ball by him. Willie is not playing for fun today, but from a sense of obligation. He has come out early so we can talk in an empty locker room, and the conversation sweeps across a goodly range. We go back a way together, and when Willie trusts you, he is warm and open and droll and humorously sly. Together, we consider divorce and alimony and child-raising and financial security and how time, the subtle thief of youth, steals from you, me and even Willie Mays.

A spring fifteen years earlier comes back in a rush, and I see again the wide pellucid sky, the baked hills wanting grass and the desert winds blowing whirls of sand. I hadn't wanted to come to Phoenix. I hadn't wanted to cover the Giants. For two previous years I'd been assigned to the Dodgers. This nurtured a condition described in a general way by the late nonpareil of sports editors, Stanley Woodward. "Baseball writers," Woodward observed, "always develop a great attachment for the Brooklyn ball club if long exposed to it. We found it advisable to shift Brooklyn writers frequently. If we hadn't, we would have found that we had on our hands a member of the Brooklyn ball club rather than a newspaper reporter. You watch a Brooklyn writer for symptoms, and, before they become virulent, you must shift him to the Yankees or to tennis or golf." Woodward was gone from the *Herald Tribune* by 1954. Still, I was shifted, under protest, to the Giants.

The ride from New York to Phoenix was interminable. We had to change trains in Chicago, wasting time, and somewhere near Liberal, Kansas, we stopped dead for ten hours in a snowstorm.

Perhaps fifty hours after we had left New York, the Southern Pacific pulled into Phoenix and we stepped out into a cool and cloudless morning. Louis Effrat of the *Times* alighted with me and looked about the station. A few Indians were sleeping. In the distance lay brown hills. "Three thousand miles," Effrat shouted. "I leave my wife, my daughter, my home and travel three thousand miles." He inhaled before bellowing, "For what?" He was making a joke, but that was the way I felt.

My outlook did not improve immediately. The Giant manager, Leo Durocher, offered me tidbits on his swelling romance with a wide-hipped actress, but was more devious when asked about the club. The ball players were decent enough, but I didn't know them, or they me, and I was starting from scratch, building up confidences and new sources. And aside from that, the team bored me. I was used to the explosive Dodger atmosphere, with Jackie Robinson holding forth and Charlie Dressen orating and Roy Campanella philosophizing. The Giants seemed somber as vestrymen.

While I struggled and wrote a story a day, plus an extra for Sunday, Willie Howard Mays, Jr. was struggling with an Army team at Fort Eustis, Virginia, hitting, as he later put it, ".470, or something like that." They were all waiting for him. The Giants had won in 1951 with Mays. Without him in 1952 and '53, they lost. Each day in the press room, one of the regular Giant writers or one of the officials would tell anecdotes in which Willie rose, mighty and godlike. In exasperation, I sat down and wrote a story for the Sunday paper that began:

"Willie Mays is 10 feet 9 inches tall. His arms reach from 156th Street to 154th. . . . He has caught everything, hit everything, done everything a center fielder can possibly do."

"Look," I told Charles Feeney, then the Giant vice president, amid the amber torrents of the Phoenix press bar. "There are a couple of other center fielders, too. Ever hear of Mickey Mantle or Duke Snider?"

Mr. Feeney erupted in song. "In six more days," he choired, to the tune of "Old Black Joe," "we're gonna have Willie Mays." He may have sung it "going to." He is a Dartmouth man.

Each day Feeney warbled, amending the lyrics cleverly enough, say, changing the word "six" to the word "five." The song, like the sandy wind, became a bane.

M-Day, as I had come to call it, dawned like most other days, with a big bright sky. Durocher scheduled an intrasquad game and began elaborately underplaying things. The loose-hipped movie star was gone, making him somewhat irascible.

"Nothing unusual," Leo announced in the lobby of the Hotel Adams early M-Day. "Just a little intrasquad game, boys, that's all." Then he walked off, barely able to keep his footing for his swagger.

The Phoenix ball park was typical medium minor league. Old stands extended partway down each foul line. A wood fence ringed the outfield. The players, Monte Irvin, Whitey Lockman, Alvin Dark, were in uniform and, as always in spring, it seemed odd to see great major-leaguers in a minor league setting.

Willie was coming by plane, we all knew that, and in Phoenix you can see great distances. Whenever an airplane appeared, one of the writers or Giant officials leaped up with a cry, "Willie's plane!" Two Piper Cubs, four Beechcrafts and one World War I Spad were positively identified as the transcontinental Constellation bearing Mays.

"Feeney," I said, "this is ridiculous."

This time he chose the key of C-sharp minor:

> In no more days,
> We're going to have Willie Mays!

The athletes were still playing catch, the intrasquad game had not started, when a trim figure in slacks and a dark open-collared shirt appeared in the dugout. He was blinking at the sunlight, mostly because he had not been to sleep, and seemed to be trying to hide, to be as unobtrusive as possible. "There's Willie," someone cried in ecstasy, and the sportswriters swarmed.

Mays stood next to Irvin, probably the closest friend he has had among ball players in a curiously lonely life. Irvin was very poised, very strong, very sensible.

"Hey, Willie," someone shouted, "what you got in that bag?"

He had dropped off his large suitcase, but clung to a smaller one.

"Not much," Willie said. "A couple things."

"What?"

"Just my glove and my jock."

Durocher hugged him repeatedly for joy and for the news photographers. Monte, who felt like hugging him, shook his hand.

"He's shaking hands with the pennant," Barney Kremenko, one of the baseball writers, proclaimed.

"Hi, roomie," Irvin said.

"Hey, Monte."

Irvin smiled. "Roomie," he said, "how's your game?"

Willie shook his head. "What you mean my game, Monte? You talking about pool?"

"No, Willie," Irvin said. "I'm talking about your game, about baseball."

"Oh, yeah," Willie said, as if surprised there should be a question. "My baseball. I'm ready any time."

A few minutes later, when the intrasquad game began, Mays remained on the bench. Durocher, with his sure sense of drama and his always brilliant sense of handling Willie, was letting the elements cook. The game proceeded without much excitement. The most interesting thing at the Phoenix ball park was watching Number 24, striding back and forth, looking at Durocher, asking with his eyes, and being ignored.

Halfway through the game, he was sent in to hit. Willie sprang from the dugout. He ran to the batter's box. He took a tremendous swing at the first pitch. His form was flawed. There was a little lunge in the swing. But I don't believe I have ever seen anyone swing harder. Three swings, and mighty Willie had struck out.

"The thing about Snider," I told Kremenko in the press box, "is that his butt doesn't fly out of there when he swings."

"Now, listen," Kremenko began, as though I had assailed the family honor. And I suppose I had.

The first unusual thing that Willie did was snatch a sinking liner off the grass. The ball came out to center field low and hard and Willie charged it better than anyone else could have and dove and made a graceful somersault and caught the ball. "Nothing," Kremenko shouted. "For Willie that's absolutely nothing."

The next time he came to bat, I resolved to look for specific flaws in his form. I was doing that when he hit a fast ball 420 feet and out of the park. An inning later, and with a man on first, someone hit a tremendous drive over Willie's head. He turned and fled and caught the ball and threw it three hundred feet and doubled the runner. Pandemonium. The camp was alive. The team was alive. And Willie had gone through the delays of a discharge, then sat up all night in a plane. I conceded to Kremenko that, given a little rest, he might show me something.

Then I sat down and wrote an account that began, "This is not going to be a plausible story, but then no one ever accused Willie Mays of being a plausible ball player. This story is only the implausible truth." It ran quite long, and I had no idea whether the *Tribune* copy desk would mince it, until a day later when a wire came from Red Smith in Florida. Red was the columnist for the *Tribune*, a thoughtful man, and his telegram, a personal gesture, was the first indication I'd had in a month that my stuff was getting printed and was syntactical.

That night Feeney, selecting the rather cheerful key of D major, honored me with the final version of his aria:

> Gone are the days,
> When we didn't have Willie Mays.

After Willie's debut and Red's wire, I was genuinely surprised to hear how much Feeney's voice had improved.

Willie conquered me. I had not come to praise him and sycophancy annoys me, but he brought to the game the outstanding collection of skills and the deepest enthusiasm to play I've seen. He was the ultimate combination of the professional full of talent and the amateur, a word that traces to the Latin *"ama-tor,"* "lover," and suggests one who brings a passion to what he does.

They used to play pepper games, Leo and Willie, sometimes with Monte Irvin as the straight man. Willie has what his father, Kitty-Kat Mays, described as oversized hands, and Durocher was one of the finest defensive shortstops. They'd stand quite close and Leo would hit hard smashes at Willie's toes, or knees, wherever. Mays' reflexes were such that he could field a hard line drive at ten or fifteen feet. And he liked to do it. He threw, and Leo slugged again. Once in a while Willie bobbled a ball. Then he owed Durocher a Coke. Durocher made great shows of cheating Willie. One morning he hit a hard smash on one hop, well to Willie's right, and Willie knocked the ball down with a prodigious lunge.

"Coke," Leo roared. "That's six you owe."

"Ain' no Coke for that," Willie said. His voice piped high and plaintive. "That's a base hit."

"Six Cokes you owe," Leo insisted.

"Monte," Willie pleaded at Irvin. "What you say, roomie?"

"Six Cokes," Irvin said, solemnly. Willie's boyish face slumped into a pout. "I'm getting the short end," the expression said, "but I'll get you guys anyway."

Sometimes Irvin hit, and then there was added byplay. Not only did Durocher and Mays stab smashes, they worked to rattle each other. Durocher seized a line drive, wound up to throw to Irvin, and with a blur of elbows and hands tossed the ball to Mays at his left. Leo has the skills and inclinations of a juggler. Willie caught the toss, faked toward Irvin, and there was the ball floating down toward Leo. Durocher reached and Mays slapped a glove into his belly.

"Oof," Leo grunted. Willie spun off, staggering through his own laughter. It wasn't long before people started coming to the ball park long before the game, just to watch pepper. The clowning would have done honor to Chaplin.

Willie ran and threw and hit and made his astounding catches, and slowly that spring I began to get to know him. I was the youngest of the baseball writers and that helped. We had little conversations after the workouts and the exhibition games, and he always became very solemn and gave me serious answers. "Who suggested," I asked one day, "that you catch fly balls that way?" The technique is famous now: glove up, near the belt buckle.

"Nobody," Willie said. "I just start it one day. I get my throw away quicker."

"Nobody taught you?"

Willie's eyes, which sometimes dance, grew grave. "Nobody can teach you nothing," he said. "You got to learn for yourself."

On another afternoon we were talking, and Ruben Gomez, a pitcher from Puerto Rico, came up and said, "Willie. That man in New York. I forget the name. I sign a paper for him."

Willie mentioned a New York agent.

"That's him," Gomez said.

"You sign a paper," Willie said, "and you worried because you haven't got your money."

Gomez nodded.

"Well, don't worry," Willie said. "Long as you sure you signed. It may come soon, or it may come late, but long as you sign something, you'll get money." He looked at me. "Ain' that right?" I thought of leases, installment contracts and overdue bank loans, but I said, "Yes." Maybe it would always be that way for Willie, spring and youth and plenty of cash and laughter. But it wasn't, not even that spring.

Along with the Cleveland Indians, a team wealthy with pitchers, the Giants flew to Las Vegas for an exhibition game late in March. The Giant management did not want the ball players spending a night in Las Vegas. The Stoneham regime is paternalistic, and the idea of a troop of young ball players abroad among the gamblers and the bosoms of Vegas was disturbing. The team would play its game with the Indians. The players would be guests for dinner at one of the big hotels. They would watch a show and seek as much trouble as they could find up until 11 P.M. Then a bus would take them to the airport for a flight to Los Angeles, where two other exhibitions were scheduled. We wouldn't get much rest.

It was a gray, raw afternoon in Vegas, and Bob Feller pitched for the Indians. Sal Maglie opposed him. My scorebook is lost, but I believe the Giants won by one run. Afterward we wrote our stories and took a bus to the hotel that had invited us all. We ate well, and I caught up with Willie in the hotel theater, where Robert Merrill, the baritone, was to sing. As I joined Willie's table, Merrill began *"Vesti la giubba,"* the aria from *Pagliacci* in which Canio, the clown, sings of having to make people laugh, although his own heart is breaking.

Merrill gave it full voice and all his passions. When he was done, Willie turned to me amid the cheering. "You know," he said, "that's a nice song."

An hour later, he was in a gambling room, standing quietly amid a group of people close to a dice table. Monte Irvin and Whitey Lockman were fighting a ten-cent one-armed bandit. Sal Maglie, glowering like a movie Mafioso, was losing a steady fifty cents a game at blackjack. I walked over to Willie. "How you doing?"

"Oh," Willie said, "I'm just learnin' the game." We both grinned.

I moved on. A stocky gruff man grabbed me by the arm. "Hey," he said. "Wait a minute."

I shook my arm free.

"That guy a friend of yours?" said the man. He pointed to Mays.

"I know him."

"Well, get him the hell away from the dice tables."

"What?"

"You heard me. We don't want him mixing with the white guests."

"Do you know who he is?"

"Yeah, I know who he is, and get that nigger away from the white guests."

If there was a good answer, except for the obvious short answer, I didn't come up with it. Very quickly I was appalled, unnerved and angry. What unnerved me was the small, significant bulge on the man's left hip.

"Do you know that boy just got out of the Army?" I said.

"That don't mean nothing. I was in the Army myself."

"You bastards invited him down to your hotel."

"Who you calling a bastard?"

We were shouting and Gary Schumacher, the Giants' publicity director, suddenly loomed large and put a hand on my shoulder. "What's the trouble?" Gary said.

"This guy," the tough began.

"I asked him," Gary said, nodding at me.

I had a sensible moment. "No trouble, Guv," I said to Gary. I took my wallet out of a hip pocket and withdrew the press card. "This joker has just given me one helluva story for the Sunday New York *Herald Tribune.*"

The hood retreated. I walked over to Irvin and told him what was happening. Lockman listened briefly and then, taking the conversation to be personal, stepped back. "Maybe Willie and I'll get on the bus," Irvin said. It was his way, to avoid confrontations, but he was also worried lest Willie be shocked or hurt.

Now a hotel vice president appeared, with a girl, hard-faced, trimly built, dark-haired. He asked if "my assistant and I can buy you a drink."

We went to the bar and the man explained that he had nothing against a Negro like Irvin or Mays playing one-armed bandits. It was just that the dice table was a somewhat different thing. As far as he, the vice president, was concerned, Negroes were as good as anybody, but he had to consider the wishes of the customers. That was business.

"We're really in the South here," said the brunette.

"I thought the South was Alabama, Georgia, Texas."

"That's it," the brunette said. "We get a lot of customers from Texas." She glanced at the bartender, and I had another drink. "We're really a very liberal place," the girl said, "even though we are in the South. We not only book Lena Horne to sing here, but when she does, we let her live on the grounds. We're the only hotel that liberal." She leaned toward me, a hard, handsome woman, working.

"Why did you invite him if you were going to shit on him?" I said. I got up and joined Monte and Will in the bus.

Later Irvin asked me not to write the story. He said he didn't know if it was a good idea to make Willie, at twenty-one, the center of a racial storm. That was Monte's way and the Giants' way and Willie's way, and you had to respect it, even if dissenting. I never did write the story until now.

In the visitors' locker at Shea Stadium fifteen years later, the headline on a folded newspaper cries out: "City College Torn by Black and White Strife." The times are different and a prominent black has criticized Mays as self-centered. It was the job of every black to work for a free society, he said. To the militant or even the mere activist, Willie is the embodiment of the well-fed, declawed Tom.

"They want me to go out on some campus?" Willie says. "Why should I lie? I don't know nothin' about campuses. I never went to college. I wanted to play ball."

"Well, what about the whole black movement?"

"I help," Willie says. "I help in my way." His face becomes very serious. "I think I show some people some things. I do it my way." He is a good fellow, serious and responsible, never in trouble, never drunk, never in jail.

"Do you speak out?"

"Like what?"

"On schools, or full employment or whatever?"

He eyes me evenly. "I don't think I should. I don't know the

full value of these things. I'm not the guy to get on the soapbox."
He pauses, then announces with great assurance and pride,
"I'm a ball player."

In the autumn of '54, after Willie led the Giants to the pennant and a sweep over the Indians in the World Series, our
paths crossed again. I was assembling a book with articles by
All-Star ball players on the qualities that make one an All-Star.
I sent questionnaires to many, like Ted Kluszewski and Bob
Lemon. I telephoned Stan Musial. I went to see Willie in the
flesh. He had made his classic World Series catch, running,
running, running, until he was 460 feet out and grabbing Vic
Wertz's liner over his head. He had taken Manhattan, the Bronx
and Staten Island, too, and was in demand. At the Giants someone gave me the name of his agent.

After hearing what I could pay, the agent said Willie would
let me have three to four minutes on a slow Tuesday afternoon,
but while we talked he might have to sign four endorsements,
accept six speaking engagements, get his shoes shined and telephone for a date. His business was being handled brusquely,
although not, we were to learn, very well.

A few seconds before the appointed minute I appeared in the
agent's office. Willie was in an anteroom, only signing endorsements. When I appeared, he waved and smiled, relieved to see
a familiar face. "Hey," he said, "Roger Kahn, is that you? I didn't
know that was you. What you want to talk to me about?"

I explained.

"You writin' a book?" Willie said. "That's real good, you writin' a book."

Disturbed by gratuitous friendliness, the agent vanished and
Willie held forth on playing center field. "The first thing," he
said, "is you got to love the game. Otherwise you'll never learn
to play good. Then, you know, don't drink, and get your sleep.
Eight hours. You sleep more, you get to be lazy.

"Now in Trenton, where I played when I first signed, I was

nowhere near as good as I am now, but I have my way to learn things. People tell me, 'Willie, do like this, like that,' but that ain't the way."

He sat in a swivel chair, which he had tilted back. His considerable feet were on a desk. "Well, how do you learn?" I said.

"Some things maybe when you're real little, you got to be told. But mostly you got to be doing it yourself. Like once I was a pitcher and now I'm in the outfield. Watch me after I get off a good throw. I look sort of like a pitcher who has thrown.

"You got to be thinking, 'What am I doing wrong?' And then you look at the other two outfielders and think, 'What are they doing wrong?' And you're thinking and thinking and trying not to make the same mistake three times, or four at the most, and you're also thinking what you'll do if the ball comes to you. Understand?"

"Pretty much."

"You don't want to be surprised," Willie said with finality.

But on what Branch Rickey called the best catch in baseball history, Mays was indeed surprised. The Giants were playing at Forbes Field in Pittsburgh, where center field ran 457 feet deep. Rocky Nelson, a left-handed hitter, smashed a tremendous line drive, and Willie, calculating at a glance, turned and sprinted for the wall. Nelson had hit the ball so hard that there was a hook to it. While Willie ran, the ball drifted slightly to the right.

At precisely the correct instant, Willie looked. He had gotten back deep enough, a mini-miracle, but now the ball was to his right and sinking fast. He might have been able to reach across his body and glove the ball. Or he might not. We will never know. He simply stuck out his bare right hand and seized the liner at the level of his knees. Then he slowed and turned, his face a great, wide grin.

"Silent treatment," Durocher ordered in the dugout. "Nobody say nothing to him."

Willie touched his cap to acknowledge the crowd and ran

down the three steps into the Forbes Field dugout. Everyone
avoided Willie's eyes. Durocher was checking the line-up card.
Bobby Thomson was pulling anthracite from his spikes. Hank
Thompson was taking a very long drink. The silence was suffo-
cating.

"Hey, Leo," Willie piped. "You don't have to say 'Nice play,
Willie.' I know that was a nice play."

A minute later a note from Rickey arrived. "That," Rickey
wrote, "was the finest catch I have ever seen and the finest
catch I ever hope to see."

I finished the story by Willie with a comment that he offered
in the agent's office. "You got to learn for yourself," he said,
"and you got to do it in your own way and you got to become
much improved. If you love the game enough you can do it."
It reads right after all the years, and true, but even as I was
finishing I understood that no book was likely to help a young
man play center field like Willie Mays.

In Shea, we start talking about the old times. "New York was
a good town for center fielders," I say, "when you were here
with Mantle and Snider."

"Yeah," he says, "Mick and I broke in together, but he had
a real bad body. Legs."

"How do you feel being the only one left?"

"Proud. Proud that I'm still playing."

"Lonely?"

"There's more new faces, but . . ." He turns his palms up and
shrugs. "That doesn't bother me none.

"I worry, though," he says. "I get worried now that I can't do
the job. 'Course I always was a worrier. I get the ball out, but
I can't get it out as often as I used to."

"About old friends," I say.

"You know," Willie says, "I don't have many friends. People
I know, people to say, 'Hi, Willie,' there's a million of them. My
friends, I could count them on a few fingers."

I went calling in 1956, four days after Willie had taken a wife. Because he is handsome and country slick, and also because he is famous and well paid, he does not lack for feminine attention. Joe Black, the Dodger relief pitcher, told me Willie was getting married. We played winter basketball together, and after one workout Joe said he hoped Willie knew what he was getting into.

"I'm sure of that," I said.

"I mean I hope he doesn't get hurt."

"What's the girl like?"

"The girl," Joe said, "is older than Willie and has been married twice before."

A number of people counseled Willie against getting married, but he doesn't like to be told how to run his life, and each bit of counsel shoved him closer to the altar. Then, in February, he gathered Marghuerite Wendelle, stuffed her into his Lincoln, and set off to Elkton, Maryland, where one can marry in haste. On the way, he picked up a $15 fine for driving seventy in a sixty-mile zone.

He set up housekeeping in a tidy brick home not far from La Guardia Airport. East Elmhurst was one of the early colonies open to the black middle class, and I remember the white taxi driver looking at the clean streets and detached houses in surprise. "Colored people live here?" he said.

Mrs. Mays received me with a cool hand, tipped with pointed fingernails. She was a beautiful woman, who stared hard and knowingly when she said hello. It was midday, but Willie hadn't come downstairs. "Just go on up," Marghuerite Mays said. "I have to go out to the beauty parlor."

I found Willie sitting in an enormous bed, gazing at morning television, a series starring Jackie Cooper and a talking dog. Willie wore tailored ivory pajamas. "Sit down," he said, indicating a chair. "What you doing now? How come you don't come around? You okay?"

I had left the newspaper business and gone to work as sports editor for *Newsweek*. The salary was better and the researchers were pretty, but the magazine then approached sports in an earnest, sodden way. A great story on Mays, my superior insisted, must explain in complete technical detail how Willie played center field.

In the bridal bedroom, I told Willie I was fine. I was wondering how to swing the conversation into a technical analysis. I asked what had made him decide to marry.

"Well," Willie said, "I figured that's it's time to be settling down. I'm twenty-four years old."

"You figure being married will affect your play?"

"I dunno," Willie said. "How am I supposed to know? I hit fifty-one home runs last year. Man, if you come to me last spring and tell me I was gonna do that, I woulda told you you were crazy." Willie shook his head and sat straight up. "Man," he said, "that's a lot of home runs."

On top of the TV set rested three trophies. The largest was a yard-high wooden base for bright gilt figurines of ball players running, batting and throwing. It bore a shiny plaque which read: "To Willie Mays, the most valuable player in baseball."

"What are you hoping to do this year?"

"I dunno," Willie said. He frowned. "Why you askin' a question like that?" he said.

I stopped and after a while we were talking about marriage. "You hear some people say they worried 'bout me and Marghuerite," Willie said. "Same people last summer was saying I was gonna marry this girl and that girl. But they was wrong then, like they're wrong now." He thumped his heart under the ivory pajamas. "I'm the only guy knows what's in here."

They didn't know what to make of my story at the news magazine. They cut out chunks of it, and devoted equal space to the picture of a 2-to-5 favorite winning a horse race. Willie's love song did not fit into news-magazine style.

The marriage went. I like to think they both tried. They

adopted a son and named him Michael, but some years later they were divorced. "Foundered on the rocks off the Cape of Paradise" is how the actor Mickey Rooney puts it, but there is nothing funny about the failure of a marriage or having to move out from under the roof where lives your only son.

In Shea before the game against the Mets, Willie is talking about the boy. "He's with me, you know," Willie says.

"How come?"

"He was with Marghuerite, but when he started gettin' older, I guess he missed me and we kind of worked something out.

"Michael is ten years old," Willie says, "and there's a lady who keeps house and she looks after him when I'm away. A real nice boy. I send him to a private school, where they teach him, but they're not too hard with him."

I think of the ironworker's son with a boy in private school.

"I've made a deal with him," Willie says. "He needs a college degree in times like these, and the deal is I send him to good schools, put it all there for him, and after that it's up to him to take it."

"You think he will?"

"He's a real good boy."

Two men have come into the Mets' clubhouse to see Willie. Paul Sutton is a patent attorney and David Stern is a vice president of Sports Satellite Corporation. Willie hopes that these men and a Salt Lake businessman named Ernie Psarras will spread his fortune to seven figures. For now Willie is concerned about filling the house he is building on an acre, in Atherton, down peninsula from San Francisco. He stands to greet Sutton and Stern and says, "Hey, what about the furniture?"

"We're seeing about it," David Stern says.

"Man," Willie says, "I got to stay on you guys."

"Willie doesn't like to pay retail," Stern explains.

"I don't like to pay," Willie says, and he laughs.

Larry Jansen, a coach who pitched for the old Giants, ap-

proaches and asks Willie about a doctor or a dentist. Willie gives
him a telephone number. Willie owns the keys to the kingdom
in New York.

When the Giants moved to San Francisco after the 1957 season, I lost touch with Willie. I read he was having problems. He
moved into a white neighborhood and a Californian threw a
soda bottle through his living room window. It was a good thing
for the Californian that Willie didn't grab the bottle and throw
it back. With that arm, he would have cut the man in half. Later,
at least as we got word in New York, some San Francisco fans
felt disappointed in Willie. They didn't appreciate him as we
had; a number said they preferred Orlando Cepeda.

I was paying less attention to sports and writing more about
other things, but I knew Willie was not disgracing himself. He
kept appearing in All-Star Games and driving homers into the
high wind over Candlestick Park. But I wondered if the years
and the franchise shift and the divorce had dampened the na-
tive ebullience.

It was 1964. Forces that would explode into Black Revolution
were gathering and an editor asked me to spend a few months
in Harlem, "a part of New York that white New Yorkers don't
know."

"I don't know it," I said.

"You've been there," the editor said.

"Sure. Whenever I took a taxi to the Polo Grounds, I'd ride
right through."

This time I got out of the taxi. I went from place to place on
foot, trying to grasp the bar of music, the despair, the life and
death, the sour poverty, the unquenchable hope of a black
ghetto. It was different from living in a press box.

To shake off the gray ghetto mood, a man can stand a drink,
and one evening I walked into Small's Paradise, with Alice my
new blonde wife on my arm. Across the bar a major-leaguer was
drinking hard, although he had a girl with him. She was quite
young, a soft off-tan, and wore an enormous round black hat.

The athlete and I raised glasses to each other's ladies. Suddenly Willie walked in.

It was a cold day in January, but his stride was bouncy. Willie wore a tailored topcoat of charcoal herringbone. He has unusual peripheral vision and he covered the bar with a glance. Then he bounced over, smiling.

"Buy you a Coke?" I said.

Willie shook his head. "How are you? You okay? Everything all right? What you doing around here? Who's the girl over there with—" And he mentioned the other major-leaguer's name.

"I don't know."

"You sure you okay, now?" Willie said.

"Fine." I introduced him to my wife.

Willie put an elbow on the bar and placed a hand against his brow and fixed his gaze at the girl. "Who is that chick, man?"

None of us knows what happened next. Willie was around the bar quickly, greeting the other ball player, talking very fast to the girl. Then he bounced out of the bar, calling, "See ya, man." Five minutes later the other major-leaguer was drunker and the pretty girl in the big round hat was gone. "That," said the blonde on my arm, "has to be the smoothest move I've seen."

Back at Shea, Willie is asking if he'd given me enough to write an article and I tell him I think so.

I find his father sitting in the dugout. Kitty-Kat Mays has his son's big grin and says, sure, he'd like to talk about the boy. Kitty-Kat is smaller than Willie. He has a round belly. He was a semi-pro around Fairfield, near Birmingham, Alabama.

"I was down there, Mr. Mays, when Bull Connor was the police commissioner."

"Things are a lot different now," Kitty-Kat says.

"You still live there?"

"No. I'm up here. I've got a good job. I work in a supermarket."

The man knows baseball, and I ask when it first struck him

that his son was going to be a superlative ball player. Kitty-Kat screws up his face, and I can see that he is going backward in time. He says, "Well, you know we lived right across from a ball field, and when Willie was eight he played with older kids."

"I mean before that, before eight."

"Soon as he started walking," Kitty-Kat says, "he's about a year old, I bought him a big round ball. He'd hold that big round ball and then he'd bounce it and he'd chase it, and if he ever couldn't get that ball, he'd cry.

"I knew he'd be a good one, with those oversized hands." Mr. Mays extends his own palms. His face twists in private regret. "I was pretty good, but my hands are regular size. Willie gets those big hands from his mother."

Willie emerges, taps his father's shoulder and goes out for batting practice. He does not take a regular turn in rotation. He hits for three or four minutes, then sits down. That way is a little gentler on the legs.

He doesn't dominate the series. The Mets do. In one game Ron Swoboda hits a 430-foot home run to left center field. Willie sprints back, the way he can, but this is not the Polo Grounds. He has to pull up short. He is standing at the fence when the ball sails out. In his time and in his park, he would have flagged it.

Later, he crashes one single to left so hard that a runner at second can't score, and then he says he wished he'd hit it harder. He hits a long double to left that just misses carrying into the bullpen for a home run. He leads off the ninth inning of a close game with a liner to left that hangs just long enough to be caught. The Giants lose three straight and, in the way of losing teams, they look flat.

When we say good-bye in the clubhouse, Willie seems more annoyed than depressed. The last game ends with the intense frustration of a Giant pitcher fidgeting, scrambling and walking in the winning run. "What can you do?" Willie says. "You got to play harder tomorrow."

We deliver

Send Newsweek for [ ] **weeks at 50¢ a week**

MINIMUM 25 WEEKS
MAXIMUM 100 WEEKS

Mr.
Mrs.
Send to: Ms. _____

Address _____ Apt. _____

City _____ State _____

Zip _____ Initial here _____

☐ PAYMENT ENCLOSED   ☐ BILL ME LATER
(Put Form in Envelope)

GOOD ONLY IN THE 50 STATES OF THE U.S.A.

73290732

Newsweek at
Half the Cover Price!

For an aging ball player, he seems at peace with himself. He went through money wildly in the early days, borrowing from the team, spending August money by April. "You're really okay financially?" I say.

"Oh, yes," Willie says. "Very good." His face was serious. "I ought to be, I've been working a long time."

Back in the Arizona spring we wore string western ties and we worried about flying DC-3s and we ate in a restaurant where a man dressed like a medieval knight rode a charger and pointed with a spear to show you where to park. Who would have thought then that the Giants would leave New York, and that my old newspaper would fold, and that in another spring, my hair showing gray, I would sit in a strange ball park and ask Willie Mays about legs; fatherhood, investments and fatigue?

As I drove home, while Willie flew to Montreal, the spring kept coming back. I saw in flashes a hit he made in Tucson, a throw he loosed in Beaumont, how Leo made him laugh, and I could hear how the laughter sounded. The racists were appalled that year. A Cleveland coach snapped at me for praising Mays and one writer insisted on betting me $20 Willie wouldn't hit .280. We made it, Willie and I, by 65 percentage points.

All this crossed my mind without sadness. Once Willie was a boy of overwhelming enthusiasm. He has become a man of vigorous pride. I don't say that Willie today is as exciting as Willie in '54, but what he does now is immeasurably harder. Playing center field at forty was beyond the powers of Willie's boyhood idol, DiMaggio, or his contemporary rival, Mantle. Willie stands up to time defiantly and with dignity, and one is fortunate to write baseball in his generation.

I thought I'd look him up again next trip.

A Jewish Education

Big, and nicely groomed, and tough, he walks past an electronic device that clatters market reports in a brokerage office in Cleveland. "Hello," he says. "How are you? Good to see you again. Let's go in here." *(Fairchild Camera up two-and-an-eighth.)*

He indicates an anteroom and leads the way with strong, easy strides. "Well," he says, "what's all this? I'm glad we could get together. I hope I can help." He pulls out chairs and sits behind a metal desk. Pipe and tobacco pouch appear. The big hands strike a match. He puffs and looks across the desk, a graying, friendly and confronting man.

Approaching fifty, Al Rosen, a successful securities executive with Bache & Company, has talked through more interviews than he remembers. When he played third base for the Cleveland Indians, he was direct and opinionated and reporters often sought him out. Now, long after the last base hit, he is not going to speak about batting or fielding or even about the prospects of Fairchild Camera. He is going to talk about what it has meant, through a life spent mostly in the elemental world of athletes, to be a Jew.

"Feel," Al Rosen says. "To me a Jew is feel." His voice is full and powerful. "The wanderings," he says, "and the searchings and the longings are in your background, and they make you feel compassion and they drive you to search for something good."

He puffs the pipe. "Compassion is fundamental," he says. "When I think of Vietnam and the inhumanities in that war and in all wars generally, even if it is one illiterate African chopping off another illiterate African's head, I get an inner sense of horror. I get a kind of outrage at the wrongness of it. I have to believe I feel this way because I am a Jew and I have a heritage that calls up horror and sadness at people hurting other people."

His face, broad and handsome, is dominated by a craggy nose that has been broken several times. He has lost some fights, but, one suspects, Albert Leonard Rosen had won many more than he has lost. He is not afraid.

His grandfather, a Polish immigrant, ran a department store in Spartanburg, on the plains of South Carolina, but soon after Al was born, the grandfather died, the store went bad and the family moved. The Rosens settled in Miami, Florida, in a neighborhood without other Jews. Rosen's father left the family when his son was eight.

"My mother had to work," Rosen says, in the anteroom at Bache, "and my grandmother took care of the house. I was a big kid, matured early, and I was working myself by the time I was eleven.

"I think of Jewish learning, sometimes. You know, with Papa standing there, a ruler in his hand, saying *Read, read, mein kind.* It wasn't that way in my house, even when my father was there. Nobody made me read. The only reason I read when I was a kid was that I had to read in school."

He cannot recall the first time he heard "Jewboy." The word was a part of his childhood. It was important for some of the other boys to call him a name. It let them show each other their audacity. *Lookit the Jewboy. Go home an' eat yuh matzos, sheeny. Come on, let's get the kike.*

"What is it?" Al Rosen asks, after more than forty years. "Is it because your nose is a little bigger, or your hair is a little curlier, or you don't go to Sunday school on Sunday morning or you're not in regular school on Yom Kippur? What is it?"

As he grew older and rougher, in Miami, Al Rosen began to spend time in a boxers' gym. He watched professionals, studying, and after a while sparring with them. His Jewish education was measured in jabs and hooks.

"I wanted to learn how to end things," Rosen says. "That was important. I wasn't starting trouble in those days, but when it came to me, I wanted to end it, and damn quick."

With his young athlete's body and the big heavy fists, and the intelligence and the courage and the drive, he learned what he wanted. He ended some fights others started, with furious speed. After that he heard "Jewboy" less frequently. It was easier, some of the others realized, to accept the Jew than to challenge him. And not only easier, but less painful.

He went out for football at a Miami high school, and after one early practice, six or seven boys piled into the coach's car. "Rosen," the coach said, "what are you doing out for football?"

"I love to play the game," Rosen said.

"Rosen," the coach said, "you're different from most Jews. Most Jewboys are afraid of contact."

He could always hit a baseball hard. Hitting was a gift within himself. By the time he was twelve he was good enough to try out for men's teams, playing the kind of softball where a beefy pitcher whips rising fast balls out of a windmill windup. There were no Jewish softball teams where he could gently learn. If he wanted to play, he would have to play among men, who hadn't known Jews, or didn't want to know Jews, or who figured that if this big, young Jewboy was gonna play with them, he better have it, and have it all. He did. In his early teens, he traveled around the state of Florida on a fast-pitch softball circuit. He was a shortstop, but what he liked most was swinging the bat.

After two years in high school, he went to Florida Military School, a prep at St. Petersburg, on an athletic scholarship. His mother was tremendously proud. He lettered in baseball, basketball, football, boxing and made the dean's list. "Some of my best friends there," he says, deadpan, "were gentiles."

It was a long time ago, before the Holocaust, and in the office, his pipe on the table, Al Rosen says that he was a big-mouthed kid. "Like most Jewish kids who grew up in a neighborhood where you had to fight," he says, "I was very aggressive and I had this chip on my shoulder and I was looking for someone to knock it off, and look, I had my share of guys who knocked it off and whom I couldn't take. But I was ready, ready for any of them. Maybe if I'd grown up in a Jewish neighborhood I would be a different guy. When you start out by having to fight all the time for your pride and self-respect, how are you gonna know when to stop?"

After the Army, he had some college, but he wanted to be a ball player. When he was struggling up through the minor leagues, there were times when he wished his name were something other than Rosen. Anything other than Rosen. Smith. Jones. Abernathy. Just not Jewish. Fighting his way up, being Jewish was just one more handicap, on top of all the other things that made it so tough to reach the majors.

He was a tenacious, dogged hitter, who stood close to the plate, challenging the pitcher. In his first full year as a Cleveland regular, he hit thirty-seven home runs. To intimidate him, pitchers threw fast balls at Rosen's ribs and head and arms. The theory is simple, and as old as baseball. A man consumed by self-preservation will not be able to concentrate on getting a hit. Rosen went down under fast balls time after time, diving for the safety of the dirt. When he got up, he stood in just as close, just as defiantly.

It hurt to be struck by a baseball traveling ninety miles an hour, but Rosen would be damned if he'd let a pitcher see him writhe. The worst pain came when the ball struck the funny bone in his left elbow. That happened twice. Each time he clenched his teeth and fought the pain and pretended it was minor. In his tweedy jacket, with his pipe, in the anteroom at Bache, Al Rosen says, "There's not a guy living who ever saw me rub."

The old Cleveland Indians were, in a baseball context, sophisticated *bon vivants* possessed of a strong team and party sense. They were not beer-drinking ball players. For the Indians, it was martinis at five, vintage wine with dinner and stingers afterward. A splendid team. The New York Yankees dominated the American League and baseball in that era, and the only club that beat the Yankees out of a pennant was the Cleveland Indians. They did it twice.

Rosen won respect from his colleagues and from players on other teams for his hard, combative style. Once, when he crouched at third base in Fenway Park, the Boston ball park, a huge, mediocre catcher began to call him names. Third base was close to the Boston dugout, and Rosen heard the names quite clearly. They were the old names, from his Florida youth.

"Time," Rosen said to an umpire. Then he started toward the dugout, where he was going to have to take on a bigger man and, team loyalty being what it is, perhaps some of the other Boston players as well. Suddenly two Boston stars, Bobby Doerr and Johnny Pesky, grabbed the catcher and convoyed him out of the dugout. Then in a runway, Doerr and Pesky shouted their contempt for a man who would cry racial epithets at as fine a professional as Rosen.

By the polished standards of the major leagues, Rosen's fielding at third base was undistinguished. But he worked hard at scooping ground balls, getting throws off quickly and charging bunts. Within a few years he grew proud of his skills. On one occasion a runner slid into third, and Rosen picked off a throw and slapped him with a tag.

The umpire spread his arms wide. The man was safe.

"No," Rosen yelled. "No, damnit. You blew it."

The umpire walked a semicircle toward George Strickland, the Cleveland shortstop. Quietly, gentile to gentile, the umpire said, "I'll get that Jew bastard one of these days."

"I'm going to tell him you said that," Strickland said.

"You wouldn't do that," the umpire said.

"I'm telling him," Strickland said, "and after he takes a belt at you, if he misses, I'm going to get you myself."

No one assaulted the umpire. All that ultimately occurred was that the umpire told some other umpires that Strickland of Cleveland was a Bolshevik, a troublemaker.

Rosen was a winning ball player, intolerant of losing and as demanding of others as of himself. Once when the Indians were about to play the Yankees, a star lay on a white table in the trainer's room, complaining of a sore muscle. "I can't make it today," the star said.

"The big man," Rosen said, "takes off against a last-place club. The big man puts up with pain to play the Yankees."

The man on the table cursed.

"Look at Mantle," Rosen said. "He plays on a worse leg than yours every day."

There was more profanity.

"I've been kidding you," Rosen said, withdrawing into formality, "and it's obvious that you're not kidding me. I think it best that you not say anything further to me and I won't say anything further to you."

Rosen wheeled and was at the door of the trainer's room when he heard, "You yellow son of a bitch."

He turned. The other Cleveland player was standing up, fists cocked. Rosen strode through punches and knocked the other ball player down. It took two men to pull him away.

Rosen fought for a lot of reasons, but he had learned to fight because he was a Jew. When he was established and a star, nationally famous, he was unhappy with his name once again.

Now he wanted one *more* Jewish than his own, perhaps Rosen-thal or Rosenstein. He wanted to make sure that there was no mistake about what he was.

An accident shortened his years in baseball. He was playing first base and a runner screened his view just before a hard drive crumpled the index finger of his right hand. He did not stay out of the line-up long enough. When he returned, pitchers threw inside fast balls so that whenever bat and ball connected, the finger was jarred. The injury failed to heal, but in the All-Star Game of 1955, with his right index finger stiff and useless, Rosen hit successive home runs. That autumn he had to retire. He retains 50 percent use of the finger.

Rosen's second career has provided security and a chance to consider values. He exposed his children to religious Judaism. Then he hoped they would decide for themselves whether to be religious. He became a suburbanite with a country club membership, addicted to tennis. But he remembers the violent years.

"A big thing about fighting," Rosen says, "is how much do you have to lose. Ten guys can terrorize a thousand. Look at the motorcycle crowd. They have nothing so they can afford to fight." He relights his pipe with the big hands in the anteroom. "I suppose the same was true of the early Nazis. They had nothing to lose."

He has thought often of the Holocaust. Certain pictures of Jews being led to death choke him with emotion. He carries the burden of being a Jew defiantly. Talking to him in the ante-room, one suspects that even now, as parent, businessman and tennis player, he would react to an anti-Semitic remark by shedding the tweed jacket, along with the broker's manner, and punching hard, to end it fast, the way he used to in Miami, Florida, so that whoever started this, and whoever was observing, would remember, next time they were inclined to pick on a Jew.

But that is only a part of the deepest consideration of his life.

"When I was up there in the majors," Al Rosen says, "I always knew how I wanted it to be about me.

"I wanted it to be, *Here comes one Jewish kid that every Jew in the world can be proud of.*"

The big, graying, broken-nosed man relights his pipe, and intensity makes the strong hands tremble.

II

Pierian Springs

In ancient Macedonia, the region called Pieria was watered by streams from Mount Olympus; Orpheus and the nine muses were said to have been born there.

A Masque
of Genius

In the end we are finding out that Shaw was right. I am speaking of the playwright, and of a time, so current and so distant, when Jascha Heifetz traveled to London as a boy of nineteen, with curly hair, a serious mien and a fiddle.

Shaw had been a music critic, a master of barbs, but hearing Heifetz overwhelmed his irascibility. Terribly moved, he went home to Ayot St. Lawrence and wrote an odd, touching, ominous letter:

MY DEAR HEIFETZ:
Your recital has filled me and my wife with anxiety. If you provoke a jealous God by playing with such superhuman perfection, you will die young. I earnestly advise you to play something badly every night before going to bed, instead of saying your prayers. No mortal should presume to play so faultlessly.

G. BERNARD SHAW

Heifetz presumed and today, robust in his seventies, he continues to play with a touch that would draw tears from an audience of stone. But such greatness exacts an incalculable price. I think that is what Shaw is saying. And Heifetz has paid for his genius with his humanity. The great violinist turns on friends and humiliates colleagues. He has lost two marriages and become remote from his children. Instead of entering an Olympian old age, his life is a hermitage. All these things are true and all are saddening. But worse, Heifetz, whose staccato is unmatched, whose legato choirs, and whose left hand flashing on the strings reminds his brightest pupil of Nureyev, refuses to give concerts any longer. He does not expect to play for an audience again.

"I have done it before," he says, as if it were that simple. "I have no need." Some suggest that Heifetz has known so many high pleasures, wealth, the smiles of queens, the adulation of an age, that he suffers from paralyzing boredom. A concert, then, is simply too much trouble. Others are not so sure. "There are only two things that go on a great fiddler," one eminent violinist says. "The bow arm and the nerve. I assure you there is nothing wrong with Heifetz's bow arm."

He practices every day. Occasionally he performs chamber music before idolatrous groups of five or ten acquaintances. He records some of the chamber music, often at a frantically rapid tempo. But what Heifetz avoids is the cut and bite and breathtaking excitement of confrontation with a real audience, which breathes and cheers and frowns. Whatever the sources, the greatest violinist in the world is now unwilling or unable to do that for which he would seem to have been put on earth. There is an irony tempered to amuse Shaw's jealous God.

Heifetz pursues secretiveness in all things. He is still trim, agile enough for wicked games of Ping-pong and capable, when he chooses, of captivating anyone with his charm. But his overwhelming passion is for privacy and he places a bewildering variety of barriers between himself and the world. Michel Piastro, who became famous conducting the Longines Symphonette, was a student with Heifetz long ago. "I'm going to the Coast soon," Piastro says. "I know that I will see Jack Benny. About seeing Heifetz, one can never tell." Musicians joke that Heifetz himself now must make an appointment to see Heifetz. ("And God forbid he should be two minutes late.")

Since his second divorce in 1963, Heifetz has lived without family or friends, in a retreat high above Beverly Hills. He spends weekends at a smaller house on a private beach in Malibu. To reach him, one may write or one may telephone his number, which is unlisted. A service answers. Sometimes Heifetz responds; invariably he refuses to identify himself on the telephone.

"Good morning," he once began a call to his associate, the distinguished cellist Gregor Piatigorsky. "What are you doing?"

"Hello," Piatigorsky said. "I was writing."

"Writing? What writing?"

"A book."

"Who do you think you are," Heifetz said, "Tolstoi?"

It is one of Heifetz's rules of life that everyone recognize his voice. It is another rule that he, and no one else, makes the jokes. He is an imperious man who has formulated rules governing every aspect of behavior, from neatness to finance to respect.

Heifetz is a fastidious dresser, fond of ascots, sports jackets, wide pants and particular outfits for particular events. To record, he changes into a tailored shirt with many pockets, which he wears outside his slacks. It is uninhibiting but dignified.

Through his sixties, he demanded and got an annual retainer of $100,000 from RCA Victor and an additional $30,000 to teach two days a week at the Los Angeles Music Center. His records no longer earned out, and he had to twist arms for his teaching salary, but he was convinced (along with many others) that both figures were fair. After all, he was Heifetz; $2,500 a week was reasonable.

His classes were conducted as absolute autocracies. "You will play the passage in this manner," he said one day, demonstrating to tall, black-haired Erick Friedman.

Friedman had been suggesting another approach. "But, Mr. Heifetz," he said, "you don't understand."

The master stiffened. "Never say that. Say, 'Mr. Heifetz, *I* did not make myself clear.'"

To discover Mr. Heifetz, one drives up Coldwater Canyon, a wrinkle in the Santa Barbara Mountains glutted with movie people. Climbing, always climbing, you turn off at a street called Lloydcrest and then again on to Gilcrest Drive. There, the Heifetz redoubt stands behind a fence of redwood saplings, and an electric gate, on which a sign warns, "BEWARE OF DOG." That is one of Heifetz's jokes on the rest of us. The beast within is a papier-mâché model of the RCA Victor puppy, listening for his master's voice.

"You had better be there when he says," John Pfeiffer, who produced Heifetz's records, suggests. "If you're early, you drive around. You really don't want to intrude. And if you're late—" Pfeiffer smiles slightly—"he won't open the electric gate." For some years, when Heifetz and Pfeiffer went to the theater together, Pfeiffer was under orders to "pick me up at 7:08."

The estate, set on about four acres, consists of a large, handsome house of redwood and glass, an octagonal studio, a tennis court and a swimming pool, where one finds another of the Heifetz signs, adorned with an appropriate arrow: THIS POOL IS FOR FUN AND PLAY; THE REST ROOMS ARE THATAWAY.

Business visitors are usually received in the studio. The building was designed by Lloyd Wright, son of Frank Lloyd Wright, with Heifetz assisting on acoustics. "He was interested," Wright remembers, "in the resonance and tone of the wood, in the various planes of sound reflections. We had a very interesting time, working out the acoustics, the serviceability, the aesthetics." This is where Heifetz keeps his violins and where he practices for the concerts he does not give. The studio is soundproof. It is immeasurably important that no one hear him prepare, that no one get behind the glacial image. When he receives a visitor, he is preoccupied with image, too.

He begins with a quick hello and an extended glare. Heifetz's cheekbones are prominent—Tatar cheekbones someone has called them—and his face is ruled by the eyes. They are blue and darting and hooded. The lips are thin and the corners of the mouth turn downward. Heifetz presents a visage that seems to say, "What is it that you want from me, and I'm certainly glad I locked the silverware." This is not a face at all. It is a mask.

Once in a while, in an old family snapshot, you can see the handsome, tender man that was. His head is thrown back. A cigarette rests on his lower lip. The face is lit with laughter. No longer. Wearing the mask has become Heifetz's norm.

One looks about the studio. There is a large monaural tape recorder. Stereo, with its stress on engineering, leaves Heifetz cold. There are files, and in a spotless case, set on a long rosewood table, *the* violin. Heifetz has owned an instrument by Stradivarius, and one made entirely of toothpicks, and one made of aluminum which, he said, "any plumber can fix." His prize is an earthy-tan violin completed in Cremona 230 years ago by Giuseppe Guarneri, a devout Roman Catholic, called Giuseppe del Gesù. The violin is signed with its maker's name, followed by a cross and the letters "I.H.S.," for "Iesus Hominum Salvator"—Jesus, the Savior of Man. This is the famous David Guarnerius, named for the German-Jewish violinist Ferdinand David, who used it to play the premiere of the Mendelssohn Concerto in 1839.

If Heifetz is not feeling depressed and the visitor has not offended him by asking questions or, perhaps, by suggesting that Mendelssohn is no match for Brahms, he may allow himself to be drawn into conversation. But talk is another kind of mask. Heifetz beats away questions with other questions and holds people off with small puns and pronouncements that are as intimate as Papal Bulls. He also has become a lover of silences.

He led one recent visitor from the studio into the breezeway, where his Ping-pong table stands, and then on to a sweep of lawn that rolls down from the main house like a meadow. It was spring, and the trees were loud with birds. "I remember spring mornings like this when I was a child in Vilna," Heifetz said.

"What was it like to grow up there?"

Silence. Heifetz had revealed more than he intended, that he was thinking of his youth. He walked off quickly to inspect one of his hammocks.

"You know," he remarked later on, "the three most important things are tolerance, humility and discipline. And I am not so sure about the third."

"But, Mr. Heifetz. Your own discipline is phenomenal."

Silence.

Other visitors are welcomed in the main house. Here one enters a small sitting room, that is dominated by an unused color TV. When TV was new, Heifetz watched for as long as five hours a day. The time waste appalled him, and he passed another rule. No TV watching at all.

Entering a larger room, one passes cases of exquisite glassware, collections from Napoleonic France and Czarist Russia. One wall, toward the meadow, is a window. On others hang paintings by Soutine and Rouault. The floor is cork. Here, before dining regally, Heifetz, Piatigorsky, Israel Baker and a few others sometimes make chamber music.

In the living room, Heifetz offers a drink. He loves bargains and he prefers a Scotch that costs a dollar less than the standard $7.25 a fifth. Then he may invite talk—animated when he describes his gardening skills, his lamp wiring and his electric car, a costly personal protest against smog. Heifetz had a Renault Dauphine converted to run on batteries. The transformation ran to $5,500. He might have done better with a Karmann-Ghia, but he will have nothing to do with things German. Gregor Piatigorsky says, "I will not play in Germany, but only because I would look over my cello and see faces and think, did this one kill a Jew or did that one, and soon I would not be able to go on." In 1946, Heifetz crossed Germany from his concert itinerary and his life. He lets such ukases stand, without comment.

Still, talking to him, as he practices conversation as a mask, can be stimulating, or at least a challenge.

"I notice that you don't have a stereo in the studio."

"Hystereo? I don't need it."

"Do you like high fidelity, Mr. Heifetz?"

"High phooey? Why should I have anything against high phooey?"

"Isn't it odd that no one has written a biography of you?"

"Here is my biography. I played the violin at three and gave my first concert at seven. I have been playing ever since."

"Don't you want a biography?"

"Why should I want a biography?"

"Have your children been musical prodigies?"

"Yes, because they were not."

"How do you feel about concertizing?"

"I have done it."

"Have some of the critics bothered you?"

"Critics are the words without the music."

"Don't you feel an obligation to bring your music to the public in concert halls?"

Silence.

"An obligation, then, to the generation of string players growing up without hearing you in person?"

"So. When I am dead and gone, will I have an obligation to them then?"

A favorite theme is equitability. "It is important," he likes to announce, "that everything is equitable." He is an artist and an individualist. He accepts only one judge of his art; that is himself. The same judge governs equitability.

A few years ago, when he was preparing films for educational television, he called Erick Friedman and asked him to participate. "I already had my own career as a soloist," Friedman maintains. "Anyway, I wasn't too anxious to appear on television as a student." But Friedman idolizes Heifetz and agreed.

"You will perform the Bach Chaconne," Heifetz said. This work, for unaccompanied violin, is one of the most difficult (and magnificent) in the literature. Heifetz's performance of it stands as an absolute in virtuosity.

"I wish I could play something else, Mr. Heifetz," Friedman said. "I haven't played the Chaconne since I was ten, and I learned the wrong fingering then."

"You will play the Chaconne."

"But, Mr. Heifetz, I'm recording the Paganini Concerto next week, and I just don't have time to work on that and the Chaconne, too."

"Very well," Heifetz said. "Play the Bach Adagio and Fugue."

Friedman thanked Heifetz. The night before the televised master class, Heifetz called. "Is the Chaconne ready?" he said.

"But, Mr. Heifetz," Friedman said, and repeated their earlier discussion.

"I remember no such conversation," Heifetz said. "You will play the Chaconne." Friedman did, with great effort, interrupted by Heifetz, who corrected him by repeating difficult passages with dazzling clarity. Equitable on this occasion was the teacher shining at the expense of the pupil.

William Primrose, an unassuming Scots-born viola player, has been an outstanding master of his instrument, which extends a fifth lower than the violin. Primrose met Heifetz in 1934, and began recording with him in the 1940s. To Primrose, Heifetz stands alone. "He has a panache, an élan," Primrose says, "that makes the simplest sonata tremendously exciting. And he can break your heart." Listening to the slow movement of the Mozart Sinfonia Concertante, a sort of double concerto for violin and viola, both Heifetz's violin and Primrose's viola sing long-lined melodies, now one following the other, now together, and if your spirit is open and you are not afraid to surrender to great art, you will find yourself moved to a sadness beyond tears.

The recording was made in 1956. A year later, Primrose began to lose his hearing, but he continued to perform with Heifetz, quietly proud of their association. The relationship ended when Heifetz and Primrose were to make a record of the Dvořák Piano Quintet. Listening to tapes, Heifetz decided that Primrose was playing out of tune. He ordered RCA not to release the recording.

Soon afterward Primrose left California and took a teaching chair at the University of Indiana. One of Heifetz's champions says, "What Jascha thought was equitable was for Primrose to come to him and say, *I can no longer play with you.* When Bill didn't, Heifetz felt he had no choice. Music is music, and long associations are irrelevant."

The affair that Heifetz sycophants find most difficult to defend ended with his loosing a sheriff on his closest friend. The late Rudolf Polk, a string player of relatively modest attainments, traveled with Heifetz, ran errands for him and testified at Heifetz's first divorce. In 1949 Polk urged Heifetz, Gregor Piatigorsky and Artur Rubinstein to form a corporation and make movies. "Unpretentiously," Rubinstein says, "we called our company 'World Artists, Inc.'" Polk, a short, intense New Yorker, became president. World Artists Corporation produced eleven short subjects. Heifetz, Rubinstein and Piatigorsky starred in two and, as principal stockholders, were to share in the profits from all. They were paid the first year, but no money remained to honor their contracts a year later.

Piatigorsky, whose wife is Jacquelin de Rothschild, dismissed the matter. Rubinstein felt that there was nothing to be done, since "We were friends, partners and, above all, artists." Heifetz handed the case to his lawyers. With Heifetz's full knowledge, while he was still playing gin rummy games with Polk, his lawyers garnished Polk's bank account and sent the sheriff to nail a writ of attachment onto Polk's house.

These stories are upsetting, but by themselves incomplete. One needs to see the other side. Dr. W. Raymond Kendall, a former chairman of music at USC, worked with Heifetz for eight years at the Los Angeles Music Center, "long enough to learn that he is tortured by a thousand demons." When the Music Center was completed, shortly before Christmas 1964, Heifetz played the Beethoven Concerto opening night. His performance, Martin Bernheimer was to write in the Los Angeles *Times,* "was a view from the summit. The tone soared with unequaled Heifetz purity. The phenomenal Heifetz technique was awesome." In short, one more apparently natural, apparently inevitable superhuman performance by Heifetz.

A few weeks earlier Dr. Kendall had come into the redwood studio unannounced. Heifetz was practicing, seated, in open-collar shirt. The score of the last movement lay open. It is a rondo, fired with insistent, quickening rhythm. Studying every note and every marking, Heifetz was playing the rondo at one-third his concert tempo. Heifetz had played the Beethoven publicly at least three hundred times. He had practiced it at least five thousand hours. He has total musical recall, and every note of every bar had fused with his being. But here at the age of sixty-three, to make sure the public performance met the Heifetz standard, he was able to discipline mind, nerves, body, spirit. He was able to practice in slow motion. I cannot think of anything more ferocious.

The stories of Polk and the others are at one with the story of his practicing. There is no way to explain such discipline because there is no satisfactory way to explain genius itself. No one really understands Heifetz's art, any more than one can comprehend how the deaf Beethoven created the late quartets or how Shakespeare sat down and wrote *Hamlet, Othello, Lear, Macbeth* and *Antony,* one after another, or how Einstein, in a little room, conceived a universe.

When we consider Heifetz, we are contemplating both a man and a phenomenon. The man is all of flesh and foibles. The phenomenon—genius—is set apart. Freud sought the keys to genius; so did Melville and Yeats, and so do contemporary geneticists. But as genius holds us, it holds us off. We establish general guidelines: drive, individualism, concentration, discipline, endurance, courage, pain. And then we stop. The sum of all these qualities does not add up to what we want. We remain on the outside looking in. As Frost observed: "We dance round in a ring and suppose,/But the Secret sits in the middle and knows."

Heifetz is a specific genius, out of a specific time and place;

close up, however, he probably brings us as close to all genius as most of us would ever care to get.

Daniil Karpilowsky, who studied with Heifetz in Russia, remembers the late Fritz Kreisler walked on stage thinking that he was performing for two thousand friends. "Heifetz," Karpilowsky says, "came out like a killer. He believed that of the 2,000 people in the hall, 1,999 had come just to hear him play a wrong note."

I can still see him walking out, on stage, in concert. He moved briskly, carrying himself very straight and with great dignity. He set his feet lightly, drew his lips back across his teeth once or twice and, with the slightest of nods, began to play. Grappling with difficult work, some violinists toss heads, shift feet, grimace, break into a sweat and fill the stage with desperate gesture. Heifetz played the most terrifying passages without change in expression beyond the arching of his left eyebrow. Nature has even endowed him with a system that does not perspire easily.

There is no way to put his sound in words. Critics have called the tone "seamless," which means that there are no breaks between upbowing and downbowing. They say it is rich and soaring and strong and virile and that it has an incredible line; that a Heifetz low G and a high E, almost four octaves apart, possess identical musical quality and timbre. Others complain that his tone is insufficiently varied, but even his detractors—and it is heady wine for a young critic to patronize Heifetz—concede that "for certain things" he is not likely to be equaled. The way to appreciate the tone is to listen to certain works where the recording has captured a significant portion of the magic. Bruch's "Scottish Fantasy" is one; the Vitali Chaconne is another, the Sibelius Concerto is a third.

His ability mystifies musicians. William Primrose says, "I hear the Mendelssohn Concerto and say, 'Ah, there's Isaac [Stern].' Then a few bars later I'd say, 'No, that's Nathan [Milstein].' With Heifetz I can always tell. He's wholly unique." Artur Rubinstein contributes that "He never missed a note and never played out of tune." Erick Friedman mentions that "As wonderful as the left hand is, the bow arm is what's incredible." David Oistrakh, the Russian virtuoso, says, "There are many violinists. Then there is Heifetz."

The violin, like a woman, has a soprano voice and, like a woman, is difficult to play well. A fiddle is constructed of spruce and maple and has, in technical terms, a waist, a button, a neck and even a back (the underside) and a belly which faces up. Four strings of catgut are stretched from adjustable pegs, across a bridge to a tail box. They are tuned to E, D, G and A. The violinist strokes the strings with a bow of horsehair, simultaneously depressing (or stopping) them with the fingers of his left hand. The point at which a string is stopped determines the note it produces. While the four fingers of the left hand move about finding stops, the right hand and arm guide the bow at infinitely variable speeds and infinitely variable degrees of pressure and at any number of angles. The necessary dexterity is such that one trains neural paths either very young or not at all. Cecil Aronowitz, one of the finest viola players in England, bemoans the fact that he did not take up the instrument until too late. "I was already twelve years old," he says.

Heifetz drew beautiful sounds from a violin when he was three. "My gen-ee-ay," his father called him after the family moved to America. Heifetz was born with absolute pitch. His hands grew into beautifully proportioned instruments. He has a supreme musical memory, and a temperament that for a long time made the handsome hands respond to the most severe demands. "It was," says Karpilowsky, "as if God took the requisites of the one supreme violinist and gave them all to a single child." Heifetz also was fortunate in the time and place of his birth.

He entered the world through Vilna, a city of 162,000, with a mountain in its center and a sense of style. "In Vilna," Isaac Bashevis Singer recalls, "there was style in houses and style in the people. Even the waiters read books."

Ruvin Heifetz, the father, was a theater violinist, scratching out a precarious living, a fiddler on the roof. Annie Heifetz, probably of peasant stock, possessed no apparent musical talent, but almost as soon as Jascha was born—it was February 2, 1901 —the father began to dream of greatness and an escape from poverty. As Jascha lay in a crib, no more than five months old, Ruvin approached playing his fiddle. The infant listened attentively. The father played dissonances. The baby wailed. Ruvin Heifetz did this many times, until he convinced himself that his new son was crowned with promise.

Before Jascha was three, his father bought him a little violin and showed him how to bow. The child responded perfectly. Then the father demonstrated simple fingering. One day, on the street, Ruvin Heifetz told Elias Malkin, the premier violinist of Vilna, "I have a genius in my house."

Malkin told Ruvin that every father thought his first-born son was a genius and that it was impossible for a three-year-old to play.

"Come," Papa Heifetz said.

As Malkin told in wonder for the rest of his seventy-nine years, "Jaschinka, with long blond curls, picked up the violin, put his eyes in the sky and played."

Four years later, Jascha performed the Mendelssohn Concerto in the concert hall at Kovno, fifty miles from Vilna. From that day onward, he would support his family, give concerts regularly and practice at least five hours every day. Before Heifetz could conquer the world, he first had to conquer Professor Leopold Auer, a supreme violin teacher, who held classes in the Royal Conservatory at St. Petersburg. Daniil Karpilowsky remembers hearing Heifetz play the first movement of the Mendelssohn in Auer's large classroom on the third floor of the stone Conservatory building during 1909 or 1910. "Afterward," he said, "I wanted to close my case and never touch my violin."

We were sitting over coffee at Karpilowsky's home in Beverly Hills. "How did his playing then compare with now?" I said.

"The same," Karpilowsky cried, in great excitement. "At eight or sixty-eight he is a miracle."

Czar Nicholas had forbidden all Jews except "Jewish artists" to live in St. Petersburg, and this presented a curious problem: Heifetz, the miraculous fiddler, was also a small boy. He needed someone to look after him. Auer, himself a Jew, enrolled Ruvin Heifetz in his class. With Papa Heifetz thus officially classified as an artist, the family was allowed to settle in the Czarist capital.

Auer was a short, bearded man given to rages. Dismissing a student once, he broke a violin over the boy's head. He taught no more than twenty people at a time, and pursued dictatorial absolutism. Everyone was required to play not only violin, but also piano and harp. Class met twice a week, and the room usually was crowded with distinguished musicians there to audit. Richard Burgin, long the concertmaster of the Boston Symphony, recalls that "We listened to each other, and we learned from each other and Auer's criticisms of one could apply to all. Except Heifetz. When Heifetz first joined, he was so young Auer addressed his remarks to the father. But as Heifetz got older, Auer spoke to him. Soon Heifetz was the one student who could get away with anything. That, Auer said, was because Heifetz 'always did everything right.' "

It took only two years for Heifetz to proceed from the class to an Alexandrian journey of triumph. He began in Berlin, which was the most vital music center on earth prior to World War I. During the winter season before Heifetz arrived, Berlin had been the site of 801 performances of opera and 1,096 other concerts.

In April of 1912, Auer described Heifetz to the Berlin impresario, Herman Fernow, saying, "In all my fifty years of teaching, I have never known such *Frühzeitige Entwicklung* [precocity]." Fernow then had Heifetz play in a private home before leaders of German musical life. Jascha stood up, one small boy before two dozen men, twenty of them violinists and nine of these soloists, and played the Mendelssohn Concerto. Pandemonium followed. Fritz Kreisler sat down at a piano and asked to accompany Heifetz in his own *"Schön Rosmarin."* "Jascha's cup runs over," Ruvin Heifetz cried. The small curly-headed boy nodded, unsmiling. What Isaac Stern calls the Heifetz era had begun.

In August of 1914, the Heifetz family was spending the summer in Dresden. When Imperial Germany declared war on Czarist Russia, the Heifetzes were interned, but with a difference. Count Helmuth von Moltke, chief of the German General Staff, had heard Jascha play. The family was installed in a spacious house with servants, and presently Moltke arranged for their repatriation through Finland. Three years later, an American impresario, Harold "Pops" Adams of the Wolfsohn Musical Bureau, offered a tour of the United States. Romantics write of the family leaving Petrograd, "while machine-gun bullets traced patterns of blood in the streets." Although one drunken Russian soldier did burst into the Heifetz apartment and threatened to shoot the three children, the Revolution had not reached its apocalypse. When the family left, Kerensky, the Social Democrat, was in power. "We were quite certain we would return," recalls one of the Heifetzes. "We left many possessions behind."

Because of the war, the journey proceeded east. The family rode across Asia in a sleeping car, and Heifetz remembers watching the sun rise over primeval Lake Baikal. Vladivostok was a ten-day trip. Then, after a shorter boat ride, and a layover in Yokohama, the family sailed for San Francisco. They finally traveled by train across the United States to New York City. The two sisters were dispatched to a relative in Massachusetts and, on the pleasant afternoon of October 27, 1917, Heifetz made the American debut of the century.

Carnegie Hall was sold out. Kreisler had been informing New York musical circles, "When I hear this boy, I want to throw away my fiddle." Heifetz, then slim, sixteen, and with fair wavy hair, walked out on the stage and began to play the Chaconne composed by the seventeenth-century Italian, Tommaso Antonio Vitali.

In form, a chaconne is a stately folk dance, three beats to the measure. Heifetz sounded the opening measures with transcendent power and assurance, and one of music's most famous witticisms followed.

"It's rather warm in here," Mischa Elman, then twenty-six, observed to the piano virtuoso, Leopold Godowsky.

"Not for pianists," Godowsky said.

The reviews were variations of the superlative. "He rose above the instrument and the music written for it," commented the *Tribune*. "A modern miracle," said the *Globe*. Sigmund Spaeth of the *Evening Mail* summed up, "He is a perfect violinist." A day later Heifetz wrote his sister Pauline in Newton. "Mama," he said, "is taking me to have a suit of tails made. Then we can go to the opera together. Isn't that exciting?" He did not mention the concert or the ovation. By sixteen he had grown as used to both as other children were used to breakfast.

Annie Heifetz, who lived until 1941, liked to tell friends she had been careful to hide reviews from Jascha "so that his head shouldn't be turned." He needed no reviews. He could hear the cries of homage and he could see people burst into tears. He was humble about his skill, but he was not long innocent of the power that it gave him over others.

The practical side, coming down from Mrs. Heifetz, neatly complemented the musical genes. Pop Adams signed Jascha for 50 concerts at $500 each, $25,000, substantial money half a century ago. But one evening Annie, considering a house of 2,000 people, each of whom paid $2 or $3, did some arithmetic. "Out of $5,000," she told Ruvin, "Jaschinka's $500 is too small." She confronted Adams with her discovery.

"Madam," Adams said, in effect, "a contract is a contract."

"Yes," Mrs. Heifetz said, "and isn't it unfortunate Jascha will be sick next Tuesday, when he is supposed to play?"

The new contract provided thousands per concert, and Jascha soon was driving an olive Cadillac roadster at high speeds. "His ambitions," observed the late Samuel Chotzinoff, his accompanist and eventually his brother-in-law, "were to excel in tennis, swimming and knowing American state capitals."

His father, short, bouncy and bald, remained a ferocious critic. Before each concert Papa Heifetz coached his son, the manager talking to the fighter. "Make the pizzicati clean. Be careful of the fingering. And not too fast, above all, not too fast." At Chotzinoff's own audition, Jascha's tempo was so brisk that the pianist could barely keep pace. Afterward Papa Heifetz berated his son, in Russian: *"Soumasetchi!"* For the American Chotzinoff he translated into Yiddish: "Mischooganer!" which means "Crazy!"

Papa Heifetz was one of the few who presumed. Berlin and New York had been taken by 1917. Shaw testifies to the fall of London in 1920. Jascha captured Paris somewhat differently soon afterward. "We were at Le Café du Père Tranquille," the playwright Marc Connelly recalls, "for a recuperative bowl of onion soup at 4 A.M., when Jascha asked the house violinist if he might borrow his instrument. As he seemed reasonably sober and able to pay for damage to the fiddle, it was handed over. Everyone quickly realized a virtuoso was present. The departing couples went back to their tables. Cooks and waiters came from the kitchen. The orchestra listened in reverence, and with the sounds of the awakening market providing a curiously sympathetic and almost orchestral background, Jascha played Viennese waltzes until the sun came through the window."

In New York, Jascha moved out on his own as soon as he was twenty-one. The family was furious. His mother wanted him to stay with her, but there was a world beyond, wild and bountiful, and, simply by doing this thing which he had done since boyhood, it was his. Jascha relished the New York life, Manhattan parties. He liked to dance and play charades and dress in costume. The suspended boyhood broke like a wave. For friends he played violin concerti on two strings and at the piano Chopin's "Étude for Black Keys," while he held an orange in each fist. Gershwin was part of his group and the painter Neysa McMein, and the pace of life was very fast and very funny. "As I remember him," Connelly observes, "he was hell-bent on getting away from restraints, and we were happy to have him, but except for his fiddling he didn't contribute very much. Of course," Connelly continues, "that's like saying that aside from writing *David Copperfield* and *Pickwick Papers,* Dickens didn't contribute much."

Heifetz was an immigrant, with ultraspecialized training, abroad in the original Smart Set. His father could accept his own ignorance without embarrassment. Once Papa Heifetz told someone: "Did you know that Beethoven wrote many symphonies? I heard one yesterday before Jaschinka played. It is not to be believed how beautiful it is." But Jascha, a generation ahead and a genius in one area, aspired to authority in all. "I'm reading *Liber Amoris* by Hazlitt," Chotzinoff once told him. "It's the precursor of *Of Human Bondage.*"

"Who is the world tennis champion?" Heifetz said.

"I don't know," Chotzinoff said.

"Borotra," Heifetz cried in triumph.

Since boyhood he had liked to be mysterious. Now, after a number of awkward contentious encounters, he developed secrecy as a shield. When he married Florence Arto Vidor, a beautiful soft-eyed movie star, in 1929, he signed the license "Jascha Cheifetz" and identified himself as "instrumentalist." It was eight days before the press discovered the marriage.

Florence abandoned her career and they set up housekeeping in an enormous apartment, decorated in Chinese modern, on top of an office building at Park Avenue and Forty-seventh Street. As adulation continued to envelop him, he looked for something simpler. He bought a rambling farm in Redding, Connecticut, and sought hobbies. He acquired rare books and began collecting stamps. Each stamp related to music, sometimes remotely. One showed Benjamin Franklin, who had played flute; others carried the Great Seal of the British Empire, which includes a harp, and a portrait of Charlemagne, who founded a school of music. Oceans and warm weather helped him relax. He built a second home near the Pacific at Balboa, California, and soon he was learning to sail.

Two children were born during the 1930s. Josepha, the oldest, lives in Mill Valley, north of San Francisco, where she is housewife and pianist, with a small career. Robert, an urbanologist, has taught at Williams College in the Massachusetts Berkshires. He plays no instrument.

Heifetz was never close to either child. By his own count he traveled around the world four times, fiddling in Ireland during Sinn Fein uprisings, in Japan, after an earthquake, in Java during rioting, in India after Mohandas Gandhi was arrested, and in Tientsin as the Japanese invaded Manchuria. "Certain things know no geographic borders," he declared. "Classical music and applause."

Sometimes Florence went with him. Often he left her behind. Musicians and critics found his performances "transcendent, effortless, sublime," but musicians and critics had said all that before. Sycophancy troubled him. He developed a persistent sarcasm, a new harshness.

After one concert a young man exclaimed with tears in his eyes, "Mr. Heifetz, you have played so beautifully, what can I say?"

Heifetz glared. "That is your problem."

He eased himself away from the New York crowd and based himself in Southern California. He made two movies, but spurned Hollywood social life. The man and the legend of the man were tending to fuse, and he began to care about the legend. Press releases emphasized not only his command of the violin but wit and regal poise. Once, a release told us, he played for royalty, drawing a warm smile from the Queen. Afterward, a courier said, "The King commands your presence at the palace."

"Certainly," Heifetz is supposed to have said, "but before the King commanded, the Queen smiled." That was what he wanted to project: a sense of a man always in cold command.

But the real man was not invisible. In 1945 he sued Florence for divorce on the grounds of extreme cruelty. "Every time we went out together in a social gathering," he testified in Santa Ana, "my wife belittled my musical abilities." Florence did not contest, and the decree was granted.

Heifetz married Frances Spiegelberg, a divorcee ten years his junior, in 1947, and soon announced that he was taking a sabbatical. "I need it," he told reporters, "and my audiences deserve it." He stayed away from the stage for twenty months. When he resumed, he played a recital before an audience that included two dozen violinists from the Boston Symphony. Afterward they brought him an unusual tribute: a large wastebasket filled with their own fiddles.

With a new beginning to his career and a new marriage, he meant for things to be different. Heifetz fussed over Jay, who was born in 1950, and read to him every night when he was home. Friends thought he was becoming more comfortable with himself. They were surprised when, after the season of 1955–1956, he decided that "I will sharply curtail my concert activity."

"Why?"

"I have been playing for a very long time."

In 1958 he tripped in his kitchen and fractured a hip. A staphylococcus infection developed, and for some time he lay near death at Cedars of Lebanon Hospital. Once he telephoned a friend and said in a rare outburst, "I have nothing to live for. I think I will go out the window."

The friend responded quickly, "You care too much about grooming. You'll never settle to finish as a blot on the pavement." The friend explains, "He was low, but I knew he wasn't serious. If you are intent on suicide, do you announce it in advance?"

Heifetz was invited to play the Beethoven at the United Nations General Assembly in 1959, and it was shocking to see him appear in the great hall. The commanding entrance was no more. To walk he had to lean on a cane. Acoustics at the UN are flawed, yet even allowing for this, the verdict of musicians was that the performance was good, but not great Heifetz. The reaction shocked him. "It was amazing," Erick Friedman recalls, "how people could hardly wait to offer consolations. And the musicians who claimed they admired him most were the first to say, never mind; they remembered how he *used* to play."

In the 1960s concerts began to make Heifetz nervous. He had seldom been tense when he played for audiences two hundred times a year, but as he withdrew and grew older, each solo performance became more of a challenge. A new fear took hold and fed itself.

The last time Heifetz played a concerto in America was on March 13, 1967. Moved by the Middle East war, he agreed to perform with the Israel Philharmonic in Hollywood Bowl. He chose Max Bruch's hundred-year-old Concerto in G minor, which contains moving passages but is not a masterwork. The Bruch succeeds or fails with the performance.

A few days before, he invited his housekeeper, Tatiana Michurina, and Miss Michurina celebrated by buying herself a new suit. As they drove to the Bowl in his gray Bentley, Heifetz kept making nervous chatter. Tatiana should wear clothing like that more often. Where had she bought the suit? It was really attractive.

"I was nothing to him," Miss Michurina says. "I was not his family. I was not his lover. I ran the house. I was a stick of furniture." Studying him as he started toward the stage entrance, Tatiana suddenly saw a face and not a mask. "He looked," she says, "stricken with fright." Impulsively, Tatiana, who is devout Greek Orthodox, clutched his arm and stroked it. "God will look after you," she promised.

The performance that followed, before seventeen thousand people, "made bravura and musicality one and the same," a critic wrote. When Heifetz had fiddled triumphantly through the last movement, a rondo with a poignant second theme, a woman seated next to Tatiana in a box embraced her, not knowing who she was. Then the woman wept at the beauty of what she had heard.

Back at the house Heifetz was weary and Miss Michurina was jubilant. "How wonderful," she exclaimed, echoing Shaw, "never to fail."

"I have failed many times," Heifetz said. He dismissed his housekeeper with a nod.

One can only surmise the ways in which he feels he has failed. The marriage to Frances ended acerbically in 1963. She testified that he had driven her from their home and changed the locks. Jay, to whom he had read, will not discuss his father. In Jay's record collection now there is nothing by Heifetz.

The teaching, successively at UCLA, USC and the Music Center, is a disappointment. Of all Heifetz's pupils, only Friedman is a soloist. The others who have remained in music are orchestral players. In Heifetz's phrase, they "contribute to the noise."

Auer, a violinist of comparatively minor attainments, had a supreme gift for selecting candidates, then for developing them, with a mixture of autocracy and warmth. Heifetz, the infinite performer, is an imperfect teacher. "He is intuitive," one famous violinist says, and it is impossible to communicate intuition.

Everyone is anxious to explain this somber, mysterious, touching man. "When he was young," says Daniil Karpilowsky, "he never had a friend, never a companion, only the family and the fiddle. It is a hard thing, not to have been permitted a childhood."

"He's very humble," says Friedman, "the way Russians are humble, and he doesn't understand the sources of his own genius. That is a part of his dilemma."

"No one understands such sources," the Russian Piatigorsky insists, in richly accented English. "No one understands how to reach such a very uniqueness."

"Without question he is a genius," says Pauline Heifetz Chotzinoff, "and always has been and has wondered about it." She is sitting in her handsome apartment directly across the street from Carnegie Hall. "But tell me, why do *you* think he he will not play?" Clues come from Heifetz himself, couched cryptically to be sure, but still discernible. "There is no such thing as perfection," he says. "There are only standards. And after you have set a standard, you learn that it was not high enough. You want to surpass it." It is lonely on the peaks, beyond most people's knowledge of loneliness. He has felt this loneliness all his life, set apart from his fellows by the sound he could make, until as the years moved past and the curls were cut and the austere lines showed pouches, he became the victim of his own genius. You and I have heard the Heifetz sound, and we expect nothing less. When it is Heifetz, we will not settle for the gifted fiddling of Isaac Stern or Milstein or Oistrakh. Heifetz knows it; he himself will not.

Inevitably, the musician, driven first by his father and then by Auer, should turn against audiences. Ruvin Heifetz and Leopold Auer are dead. We audiences have become the demanding ones. We demand superhuman playing, after which some of us may even find fault. *Wasn't the adagio somewhat brisk?*

Beyond his responses to others, there is something else, inner and supremely private. The Alexandrian journey is done, and Heifetz is embarked on the one campaign even he cannot win. He is waging the struggle of genius against old age. We know the end; so, one is certain, does he. I miss his playing, but he has the right to do battle against lapsing concentration, slowing fingers, faltering nerve, in privacy, unobserved and unheard. The contest now is between the man and his mortality.

What he enjoys these days, as much as he still enjoys anything, is a weekend by the Pacific at Malibu. There he puts on a floppy hat and makes a drink or two and plays the records of a fat-toned jazz pianist on a $90 phonograph. The very mediocrity appeals to him. That and the sea. His lifetime has been matched to tempi. At last, the changing, constant sea-rhythm consoles.

As one sits with him in the pink house at Malibu, it is almost possible to forget that this is a genius whose humanity has been sacrificed on an altar of perfection. But then he will suddenly cry, "All right. Go out please and walk." Then Jascha Heifetz closes the windows, draws the blinds, clamps a mute on the Guarnerius and, having made certain that no human can hear him, the greatest of all violinists begins to play.

Encountering Frost

To find Robert Frost, the great poet who wrote so fondly of New Hampshire, one drove deep into the Green Mountains of Vermont. The paradox amused Mr. Frost. It made his green eyes twinkle and moved him to soft laughter. Beyond his eighty-fifth birthday, Frost wore the seasons lightly and humor ran strong and young within him.

If America anointed Poets Laureate, Robert Frost, of course, would have been chosen. His poems won him four Pulitzer prizes, a special Congressional medal and, more important, earned for him and the craft of poetry the admiration of millions who found Pound, Stevens, Eliot, obscure and puzzling.

"I never like to read anyone who seems to be saying, 'Let's see you understand this, you damn fool,'" Frost said. "I haven't any of that spirit and I don't like to be treated with that spirit." The spirit Frost did possess, scholarly, independent, questioning, sage, reached out, a golden beacon across an uncertain land.

What sort of talk did one hear on paying Frost a visit? Talk about poetry, to be sure; good talk that stirred the mind. But more than that, one heard about scores of other things: Fidel Castro's revolution and John Thomas' high jumping; the feel of farming and the sight of beatniks; loneliness and love and religion and Russia, and how important it is for a man to know how to live poor. Somewhat sadly, too, one heard about the Boston Red Sox. Frost rooted for the Red Sox, but cheerlessly. He felt that they played baseball in the manner of Boston gentlemen and, although Frost appreciated Boston gentlemen in their place, he did not feel that their place is on a ball field. "Spike 'em as you go around the bases," he suggested.

Frost was not a poet by accident, and much of what one heard came in phrases which, like his poems, were vivid and exciting. It was not surprising to find here such sure command of English, but what may surprise you is the freshness with which the patriarchal Frost looked at the world. He once wrote:

> I never dared be radical when young
> For fear it would make me conservative when old.

At eighty-six he was neither radical nor conservative. He was simply Robert Frost, one man unique in his time and in ours.

Come with me then backward in time to the year 1960 on a cool, pleasant afternoon when Vermont summer is changing into fall. The route, up from the south, leads past mountains and farmland almost into Middlebury, the college town. Then you turn off the main highway into a side road that runs through the village of Ripton and, for a time, follows the course of a swift-running stream. A few miles beyond Ripton, approaching a spine of the Green Mountains, you turn down a dirt road, and when the dirt road stops, you get out of the car and walk up to the brow of a hill. There, in an unpretentious house of weathered timber, Frost lives by himself.

Two old friends, Mr. and Mrs. Theodore Morrison, occupy a large farmhouse at the bottom of the hill. Morrison is a novelist and a member of the English faculty at Harvard. Mrs. Morrison is unofficial secretary to Frost, handling his correspondence, screening visitors, helping the poet with such mundane matters as income-tax returns. The Ripton farm is Frost's home from May until October. During the winter he lives by himself at Cambridge, Massachusetts, when he is not traveling to recite and talk about poetry.

"Are you going to use a tape recorder?" Mrs. Morrison asked in the farmhouse. She is a sprightly, cultured lady who has been close to, and perhaps suffered, writers for most of her life.

"No, I thought I'd set up my typewriter and just type as he talks."

"Good," Mrs. Morrison said. "He's had a lot to do with tape recorders, and he doesn't like them very much. He feels they make one watch every word, make every word permanent, whether it's really meant to be permanent or not. Come. Let's start up the hill."

Entering Frost's home, one walks into a small, screened porch. The porch leads to a rectangular living room, with a stone fireplace in one long wall and a window, opening onto the countryside, opposite. Above the hearth, two red roses sat in tiny vases. "We're here," Mrs. Morrison called.

Frost emerged from the bedroom, walking very straight, and shook hands firmly. He was wearing blue slacks, a gray sweater and a white shirt, open at the throat. He is not tall, perhaps five feet seven, but his body is strong and solid as one might expect in a man who has spent years behind a plow. His hair, once red, is white and luxuriant. His face, with its broad nose and resolute chin, is marked by time, but firm. It is a memorable face, mixing as it does strength and sensitivity.

"No tape recorder," Mrs. Morrison said.

"Good," Frost said. "Very good."

Mrs. Morrison helped set up my typewriter on a table she uses when taking dictation and excused herself. The poet walked to one of two large chairs in the room and motioned for me to sit in the other. "You're a journalist?" Frost asked.

"Yes, mostly. I write a few other things, too."

"Nearly everybody has two lives," Frost said, smiling. "Poets, sculptors. Nearly everybody has to lead two lives at the least."

"What life have you been leading recently?" I asked. "What have you been doing?"

"I never am doing anything, really," Frost said, "and I can't talk about my plans until I see how the plans work out. If I were writing a novel or an epic, I could tell you what I've been doing, but I don't write novels or epics.

"I don't have any routine," Frost said. "I don't have any hours. I don't have any desk. I don't have any letter business with people, except I dictate one once in a while. Lectures? Lecture is the wrong word. I'm going to about twenty or twenty-five places from here to California, but lecture is the wrong word. I talk, and then I read. I never wrote out a lecture in my life. I never wrote a review, never a word of criticism. I've possibly written a dozen essays, but no more. You couldn't call mine a literary life." Frost chuckled and gestured at the typewriter.

"You use that thing pretty well," he said.

"Thanks," I said.

"Never learned to type, myself," Frost said.

"The world," I said. "Khrushchev and Castro—what do you think about what the world's been doing lately?"

"I wonder," Frost said, "if God hasn't looked down and turned away and said, 'Boys, this isn't for me. You go ahead and fight it out with knives and bombs.' "

Frost runs a conversation as a good pitcher runs a baseball game, never giving you quite what you expect. There are semihumorous answers to serious questions and serious answers to semihumorous questions. Frost is a master of the conversational change of pace.

"The world," he said, earnest now, "is being offered a choice between two kinds of democracy. Ours is a very ancient political growth, beginning at one end of the Mediterranean Sea and coming westward, tried in Athens, tried in Italy, tried in England, tried in France, coming westward all the way to us. A very long growth, a growth through trial and error, but always with the idea that there is some sort of wisdom in the mob. Put a marker where the growth begins, at the eastern end of the Mediterranean, and there's never been a glimmer of democracy south of there. Over east, in Asia, there have been interesting ideas, but none bothered by the wisdom of the mob.

"Our democracy is like our bill of fare. That came westward, too, with wheat and so on, adding foods by trial and error and luck. I think, when corn comes in good and fresh, what would I have done if Columbus hadn't discovered America?" Again the change of pace.

"What is this Russian democracy?" Frost said. "Ours, I say, is like our bill of fare, kills a few people every year probably, but most of us live with it. The Russian democracy is like a doctor's prescription or a food fad. That's all there is to that. That finished them off." Frost laughed.

"I have pretty strong confidence that our kind of democracy is better than a trumped-up kind," he said. "I'm pretty sure we're going to win. I'm on our side, anyway."

After Boris Pasternak, the late Russian poet and novelist, won the Nobel prize for *Dr. Zhivago,* but was prevented by commissars from accepting the prize, Frost was asked to issue a personal protest. "I couldn't do that," he said. "I understood what it was he wanted. He wanted to be left alone. He could have gotten out and gotten the [Nobel prize] money, but he didn't want to. He had done what he wanted. He'd made his criticism. He lived in a little artists' colony outside of Moscow, and that was where he wanted to live and be left alone, and I had to respect that. I'm a nationalist myself."

Frost paused then to ask a question. "Have you noticed," he said, "that every bill up before Congress lately, bills on horses, men, everything, winds up: 'This would tend to promote international peace'?"

It was a short hop from Pasternak and Khrushchev to Castro. "I'd be in favor of leaving Castro alone for a time," Frost said, "and seeing if he can make it. We've gone past the time when we can fight to protect foreign investments. You know what I'd do? I'm protected up to $10,000 on what I put in the savings bank. We could protect anyone who wants to invest in foreign countries up to half a million. A sort of insurance. Then we beg these investors to behave themselves. Try to make friends. Explain to Castro, 'I want to help you help me and your people make money.' If that doesn't work, pack up, come home, prove your failure and collect your insurance."

The idea delighted Frost. "I'm going to propose that," he said, "the next time I'm in Congress. The general policy of the past—backing foreign investments—is over. Protect them with insurance, but not with army, navy and diplomacy. That doesn't work any more.

"Belgium was the most selfish of all nations. They're getting their reward for that in the Congo now. England was a little loftier. The English brought nice Indian boys back to Oxford to see what freedom was. Castro is a puzzle to me, but he ought to see that we are a well-meaning nation. He needn't blackguard us all the time."

Frost placed one hand before his eyes, and when he spoke again, his voice was very soft. "Unfinished business," he said. "I'm very much in favor of unfinished business. Some of them aren't, but every single heading in the newspaper represents a whole lot of things that have got to stay unfinished, that can't be finished. Us and Russia, that might take a couple of hundred years before it's finished. That's one of the hard things about dying, wondering how the unfinished business will come out.

"Oh, you could go crazy with too much unfinished business. You'd feel unfulfilled. You make a finished article out of this, and I make a finished poem. But take anyone's career. That has got to be suspended and thought a great deal, and you're not saying much about it till you see how it comes out. You suspend judgment and go to bed."

Outside, beyond the window, a lawn stretched down the hill. To the far right lay a brown field, newly turned by the plow. Beyond the valley, mountains rose, deep green. "Three things have followed me," Frost said. "Writing, teaching a little and farming. The three strands of my life."

"About writing," I said.

"A boy called on me the other day and said, 'I'm a poet,' " Frost went on. "I said, 'That's a praise word. I'd wait until somebody else called me that.' " Frost laughed a little now. It had been a long and lonely time before many people called Robert Frost a poet.

"I started by the ocean," Frost said. "San Francisco. My father was a newspaperman there. He went to Harvard, finished first in his class, but he never talked much about that. Once he got West he put the East behind him, never mentioned it, drank enough for three generations of Frosts, died young. My mother was born in Scotland, raised in Ohio."

"Did you grow up amid books?" I asked.

"Didn't you? Didn't you?" Frost said, his voice almost a chant. "Oh, I never got the library habit much. I have an interest in books, but you couldn't call me a terribly bookish man."

There are two bookcases in Frost's living room, and on the window seat between our chairs books rested in three small stacks. His recent reading ranged from Latin poetry to a work about contemporary architecture. But the room was not over-run with books. The average publishing-house editor lives among more books than does Robert Frost.

"We came to southern New Hampshire after my father died," Frost said. "I escaped school until I was twelve. I'd try it for a week, and then the doctor would take me out. They never knew what the matter was, but I seemed to be ailing. I got so I never wanted to see school. The first time I liked it was in New Hampshire. I liked the noon hour and the recess. I didn't want to miss what went on then, and so I became interested in the rest of it, the studies.

"It was a little country school. There was no grading. I could go as fast as I wanted, and I made up the whole eight years in a year and a half without realizing I was doing it. Then they sent me down to Lawrence [Massachusetts] to live with my grandfather and go to the high school where my father had gone. It was just the luck of that year in the country, that country school. Otherwise, I might not have made it.

"In high school I had only Greek, Latin and mathematics. I began to write in my second year, but not for any teacher. There were no English teachers. We had an active school magazine that the teachers had nothing to do with. I must have been reading Prescott's *Conquest of Mexico,* because my first poem was a ballad about the night the Indians fought Cortez. People say, 'You were interested in Indians the way children are interested in cops and robbers.' But it wasn't that way at all. I was interested in Indians because of the wrongs done to them. I was wishing the Indians would win all the battles.

"The magazine would surprise you if you saw it. We did it for pleasure. When they do it nowadays, they have teachers, and that spoils the whole thing. They say, 'I can't finish this, teacher, help me.' That spoils it. We had poems, stories, editorials, and we did it all ourselves. I edited the magazine the last year, and I had eighteen assistant editors. One day I got mad at them. They weren't giving me enough material. I got sore and went down to the printing room, and in a day or two I wrote the whole damn thing. I wrote it all. I even made up a story about the debating union and wrote the whole debate. I wrote it all, the whole thing, then I resigned." Frost smiled at me as he remembered something he had done seventy years before of which he was still proud.

"Dartmouth is my chief college," he said, "the first one I ran away from. I ran from Harvard later, but Dartmouth first. In a little library at Dartmouth I saw a magazine, and on the front page there was a poem. There was an editorial inside about the poem, so evidently that magazine was in favor of poetry. I sent them a poem, "My Butterfly." It's in the big collection. They bought it so easily I thought I could make a living this way, but I didn't keep selling 'em as fast as that. The magazine was called the *New York Independent,* and after they bought the poem they asked that when I sent them more, would I please spell the name of the magazine correctly. I'd made a mistake, but they bought my poem.

"When I told Grandfather Frost I wanted to be a poet, he wasn't pleased. He was an old-line Democrat, the devil take the hindmost, and here I was, making good grades, and wanting, he thought, to waste my life. 'I give you one year to make it, Rob,' he said. I put on an auctioneer's voice. 'I'm offered one, give me twenty, give me twenty, give me twenty,' I said. My grandfather never brought up poetry again."

Frost married Elinor White, his co-valedictorian at Lawrence High, in 1895, and set about rearing a family and dividing his life among poetry, teaching and farming. "I had to find other means than poems," he said. "They didn't sell fast enough, and I didn't send my poems out much. Oh, I wanted them to want my poems. Some say, 'Do you write for yourself entirely?' 'You mean into the wastebasket?' I say. But I had pride there. I hated rejection slips. I had to be very careful of my pride. Love me little, love me long. Did you hear that? Were you brought up on that? Love me little, love me long." Frost smiled. "But not too little," he said.

He placed a hand before his eyes again. "One of the most sociable virtues or vices is that you don't want to feel queer. You don't want to be too much like the others, but you don't want to be clear out in nowhere. 'She mocked 'em and she shocked 'em and she said she didn't care.' You like to mock 'em and to shock 'em, but you really do care.

"You are always with your sorrows and your cares. What's a poem for if not to share them with others? But I don't like poems that are too crudely personal. The boy writes that the girl has jilted him, and I know who the boy is and who the girl is, and I don't want to know. Where can you be personal and not in bad taste? In poetry, but you have to be careful. If anybody tries to make you say more—they have to stop where you stop.

" 'What does this poem mean?' some ask.

" 'It means what it says.'

" 'I know what it means to me, but I don't know just what it means to you,' they say.

" 'Maybe I don't want you to.' "

Frost was sitting back comfortably, his mind at work. "We have all sorts of ways to hold people," he said. "Hold them and hold them off. Do you know what the sun does with the planets? It holds them and holds them off. The planets don't fall away from the sun, and they don't fall into it. That's one of the marvels. Attraction and repulsion. You have that with poetry, and you have that with friendships."

For a time in his youth, guarding his pride, developing his art, Frost expected to work as a New England farmer for the rest of his life. "But people asked me out to read," he said, "and that kind of checked that. Then, when I was teaching in academies, having a successful time, it would be eating me all up, taking me away from poetry too much. Whenever it got like that, I'd run away.

"I didn't have any foundation to help me, but I had a tiny little bit of money saved up, and I went to England. Not for the literary life. I didn't want that. But we could live cheaper there. The six of us [including his wife and four children] went to England, and we stayed for three years for thirty-six hundred dollars, fare and everything. We lived poor, but we had a little garden, and we got something out of it, and we had some chickens. We lived very much like peasants. I was thirty-six years old or so, and I'd never offered a book. My poems were scattered in magazines, but not much. Then one day I thought I'd show a little bunch of poems. I left them with a small publisher, and three days later I signed the contract. Funny, it had never occurred to me to try a book here. *A Boy's Will*, that was the book."

This was a time when beatniks, masquerading as poets, recited their work at you, pinning you to the ground when necessary. Frost, mentioning his first book, which brims with classics, offered no recitations. Only when I urged him did he nod. Then, looking at me intently, he spoke this stanza from his poem "Reluctance":

> Ah, when to the heart of man
>   Was it ever less than a treason
> To go with the drift of things,
>   To yield with a grace to reason,
> And bow and accept the end
>   Of a love or a season?

He spoke his poetry surely, clearly, with perfect command of the cadences. It is poetry written to be heard aloud, and when you heard it in Frost's voice, you felt that it reached its final measure of beauty in those fine New England tones.

"I once thought I'd like to have my lyrics seen as well as heard," Frost said. "I had some booklets made up and given out to audiences who came to hear me. That lasted two nights. The second night so many wanted me to sign the booklets that the police had to get me away. Now I sign anything of mine that they type out or write out. Without money and without price, you see. There's quite a little of that in me."

After Frost returned from England with his family, he had to go back to farming and teaching. He was forty before he gained much recognition as a poet, and he was nearly fifty before his volume *New Hampshire* won him his first Pulitzer prize. It struck me then, sitting in the little living room, that Frost has gone from complete obscurity to great fame without changing his way of life. The Vermont house was as simple as the houses where he dwelled when there was no choice but to live simply. One difference is that by 1960 a sizable portion of the world had tried to beat a path through the woods and up to Frost's door.

"You have to be careful about idolizers," Frost said. "Emerson calls an unwanted visitor a devastator of a day. It's a cranky Yankee poem, but I suppose he was pestered all the time by people who wanted to go deeper into him than he could go himself, and, goodness, he was such an artist they should very well have left it where he did. They think, the idolizers, that you've injured them. Whether they injure you or not, the idolizers always think you've injured them.

"How much do you need someone who always thinks you're a hero? How much do you need being thought a hero all the time? People say, 'I got over this, I got over that.' They are a lot of fools, the people who say you get over your loves and your heroes. I never do. I don't change very much."

"Has your method of writing changed?"

"If I'm not in shape so I can strike it out, like a good golf stroke or a good stroke of the bat, there's not much I can do," Frost said. "Oh, you get so that some days you can play a beautiful game, but there are always days when you can't. Those days, I can't redo them. They're done. Down the sink.

"What some seem to do is worry a thing into shape and have others worry with them. Not to say I don't have the distress of failure, but the worry way isn't for me. There are the days you can and the days you can't, and both are training toward the future days you can. Do you know the story about how the bear is born?"

I didn't.

"The bear is born shapeless, says the story, and the mother licks it into shape. That's the way it is with some people's writing. But no good piece is worried into shape. A child is unfortunate that needs to be reshaped just after it's born. Is a poet made? A poet might be through all the years of trial and error, but any good poem is not made. It's born complete."

In many of Frost's poems, loneliness is a strong theme. His wife died in 1938, and only two of his five children survive. I wondered how he had come to terms with solitude.

"In the big newspaper office," Frost said, "where everyone sits alongside the other and writes—I couldn't do that. Even reading. I've got to be totally absorbed when I read. Where there are other people reading, too, I don't feel very happy.

"Alone you take all your traits as if you were bringing 'em to market. You bring them from the quiet of the garden. But the garden is not the marketplace. That's a big trouble to some: how you mix living with people with not living with people; how you mix the garden with the marketplace.

"I like the quiet here, but I like to have a big audience for my talks, to have a few turned away. I like to feel all that warmth in the room. At Kansas City once they told me, 'You see that hazy look down the end of the hall. That's whiskers. Them's beatniks.' They came and I wish 'em well, but I do like some form in the things that I read."

Suddenly Frost sat up straight. "I'm sorry I can't entertain you," he said. "I'm not set up here for that sort of thing."

He meant drinks, and I asked if he took a drink himself.

"A daiquiri once in a while," he said, "but not much, and not serious. I don't care for those parties where everyone does. They take just a little too much, and they say just a little too much. I've always been shy. I get uncomfortable."

Outside, in the late-afternoon sun, the grass looked bright and fresh. "Used to play softball out past there," Frost said. "I pitched. They don't let me do all the things I want to any more, but if we had a ball, I'd pitch to you a little, and I'd surprise you." He grinned.

"You like sports?"

"Oh, yes," he said. "You get a certain glory out of being translated, but no, no, it doesn't work. So much is lost. There are other arts that are international. Boxing, and high jumping seven feet two inches. Anyone can understand that. Just think of that boy from Boston [John Thomas] going right up in the air higher than anybody but a basketball player."

Then we were serious again, and I asked about another strong theme in Frost's work, the theme of God. "Don't make me out to be a religious man," Frost said. "Don't make me out to be a man who has all the answers. I don't go around preaching God. I'm not a minister. I'm always pleased when I see people comfortable with these things. There's a rabbi near here, a friend of mine, who preaches in Cincinnati in the winter. He talks at the Methodist church here sometimes and tells the people in Cincinnati that he's a summer Methodist.

"People have wondered about him at the Methodist church. One lady was troubled and said to me, 'How do they differ from us?'

" 'What you got there on that table?' I said.

" 'That's a Bible,' she said.

"I didn't say any more.

" 'Oh,' she said. 'Oh, the Old Testament. Why can't you have a Jew in church?' she said, and she understood."

Frost's voice was strong. "There's a good deal of God in everything you do," he said. "It's like climbing up a ladder, and the ladder rests on nothing, and you climb higher and higher and you feel there must be God at the top. It can't be unsupported up there. I'd be afraid, though, of any one religion being the whole thing in one country, because there would probably come a day when they would take me down to the cellar and torture me—just for my own good."

He smiled briefly. "There is more religion outside church than in," Frost said, "more love outside marriage than in, more poetry outside verse than in. Everyone knows there is more love outside the institutions than in, and yet I'm kind of an institutional man."

We turned back to poetry then. "They ask me if I have a favorite," Frost said, "but if a mother has a favorite child, she has to hide it from herself, so I can't tell you if I have a favorite, no."

"Is there one basic point to all fine poetry?" I asked.

"The phrase," Frost said slowly, clearly, "and what do I mean by a phrase? A clutch of words that gives you a clutch at the heart."

His own phrases, his own words, were all about me in the little house. Afternoon was fading, and I realized how much we had discussed; and how Frost had ranged from the profound to the simple, as his own life, which seems so simple, has in reality been so profound. I remembered his poems, too.

Some summing up seemed in order and, for want of a better term, I intended to say that this visit had brought me into the presence of greatness. "I feel as though—" I began.

"Now, none of that," Frost said, anticipating. "We've had a fine talk together, haven't we? And we've talked to some purpose. Come now, and I'll walk with you down the hill." He got up from his chair and started out the door and down the steep path, pausing to look at the sunset as he went.

II

Frost wrote many kinds of poems about many kinds of things and he resented all attempts to explain or to restate what he had labored to produce. Once, when someone plagued him to "please explain that poem," he remarked, "Do you want me to say it in worse English?"

I think I knew him well enough to disqualify myself as a critic. A fine immediate criticism was written in London many years ago by a man who was killed in the First World War. "These poems," Edward Thomas commented of *North of Boston*, "are revolutionary because they lack the exaggeration of rhetoric." Final criticism may still be premature. Was Frost, as he himself liked to suggest, a culmination of New England culture, an end product of Longfellow, Emerson and a hostile soil? Or was he a precursor? Or was he both? As I say, answers are premature. Many argue today whether Mozart crowned Haydn or created Beethoven.

Many were confused by Robert Frost. They saw him as a gentle New Englander, which he was not. They saw him as a simple farmer, who wrote simple poems, which he did seldom. They saw him as a placid figure, forgetting, because he did not remind them, that his art, like his life, was wrought of restlessness and torture, as well as moments of controlled delight.

"You can quote me on anything," he once said, "except writers and writing."

"Why?" I asked.

"Because," he said, triumphantly, "I'm not a critic."

That was his pride, a pride ferocious.

I think it is fair now to report some of our talk about writers and writing; fair and important because his words should be preserved. This was not idle talk. It built toward a philosophy.

"When I went to England, mostly unpublished, I took a bunch of verses down to a little publisher in London—not a vanity press, mind you—and he liked them and he printed them. I'm not a literary man, but after that they wanted me to join the literary life and asked me to a group that Pound ran.

"Economy. That was what Pound wanted. I write a poem and give it to you; you write it in fewer words. Six people sitting around a room, writing poems in fewer words. Pound said, 'Got a poem on you, Frost?' I pointed to my head. 'Up here.' I wrote it out and picked up a magazine:

> Sea waves are green and wet
> But up from where they die
> Rise others vaster yet
> And these are brown and dry.
>
> They are the sea made land
> To come at the fisher town
> And bury in solid sand
> The men she could not drown.

"Pound came back in a little while. 'Don't have too much on you, Frost. Took you forty-five words. Best I could do was forty-two.'

" 'Yes,' I told him, 'and destroyed my rhyme and destroyed my meter and probably destroyed my sense.' "

We were sitting in the cabin where Frost liked to spend his summers. Our chairs were pushed close together. Frost jabbed an elbow into my ribs. "That settled Pound's hash," he said. "He never tried to tell me how to write poetry again."

He was fiercely proud of his art long before Presidents and college professors knew that the art existed, and he kept his pride, very much as it was, through all his years. He rejected Pound's advice and Pound's way, but because Frost was, as he put it, "for poetry," he never rejected Pound. He visited Pound at St. Elizabeths Hospital in Washington. Afterward, he summoned Sherman Adams and said that Pound ought to be freed.

"It is wrong to imprison poets," Frost said, explaining, later, "but since he's been free Pound has been writing me unpleasant letters. Scatological. He keeps using the word 'shit.' "

From Frost, the word shocked. My mouth fell.

"But that's not the worst thing," Frost said. "The worst is what he's doing to Eliot. He writes Eliot and says, 'I was wrong about you. You're not a good poet.' "

Frost cared about his guests; he was a gentleman. One does not leave guests shocked.

He believed, as did Shakespeare, in the sound of words, in the immediacy of the phrase, in the transcendent fact of rhythm. "Could you ever teach rhythm?" I asked him once, as we stood on the hill near sunset.

"No," he said, touching his ear. "It's either there or not."

"That cheers me," I said, "because my son is three and listens to Elizabethan lyrics and doesn't understand the words."

"Three years old and responds to rhythm, you say?"

"Yes."

"Of course," Frost said, "because his heart beats and he's seen the waves."

So he was—and nothing else is as important—a lyric man who loved beauty and who moved with beauty and who spoke with beauty, wholly original and unique.

I brought my son to see him a year later, on a day when Frost wanted to talk politics. I listened, disappointed. I wanted to talk writing. The child ran out into a cornfield and played. Then it was time to go and I gathered the child, hiked him onto my shoulder and started down the steep hill. Frost ran to the porch, calling, "The boy, the boy. I have to say good-bye to the boy." I turned and then the boy stared at Frost, who was eighty-seven, stared at Frost, all wonder, and Frost looked at the boy with a face I read as love.

Down the hill, I heard Robert Frost cry after me, "Come back again, if you'd care to." Because trivialities crowded my time, I never did.

The Thorns
of Glory

In the garden, beyond a shimmering willow, the great pianist weeded on his knees, ripping cattails out of rocky Vermont soil. Then, striding before a small procession of visitors, a blowzy housekeeper appeared. "Stop now, Don Clow-dio," the woman called in the dictatorial tones of Old World servants. "People are here to see you."

Claudio Arrau, the virtuoso, wore a workshirt and wide corduroy trousers. He looked, climbed up from his knees, smiled.

"Maestro," cried a visitor who is one of his managers, "you're gardening without gloves. Think of sharp stones, poison ivy, snakes. Your hands!"

Arrau shrugged and spread green-stained hands before his face. The hands are wide—he spans eleven notes between thumb and forefinger—wide, pliant and youthful although he has entered his seventieth year. "But I never worry about my hands," Arrau said, in a soft, musical way. "For a pianist to become obsessed with hands is one more way to neurosis, paralysis, even madness."

The servant scurried back toward a white clapboard summer house, and as the party strolled in dappled July sunlight, it was the virtuoso who now led. "Hands play the notes," Arrau said, "but music is more than notes. Is poetry only the words, only the letters? Music is the yearning of Brahms, the tragic passion of Robert Schumann, the trembling of Beethoven's soul." A breeze rustled the willow. Arrau's voice was very low. "To make that music," he said, "I play not with my hands but my psyche and my life's blood."

At the age of sixty-nine, Claudio Arrau, trim, agile and bursting with ebullience and youth, was giving a hundred concerts a year. His musical memory remained so extraordinary that he would have had to play seventy-six different recitals of two and a half hours each to run through his solo repertoire. His dexterity literally dazzled the eyes. Watching Arrau play the concluding fugue of Beethoven's fiery, tormented *Hammerklavier*, one saw the hands only as blurs. But Arrau, like Beethoven in late years, had surpassed technique and transcended flamboyance.

From the beginnings of his memory, in the first years of the twentieth century, Arrau studied Bach, Mozart, the great masters, first learning their pieces individually, then studying each piece in relation to the composer's other work and finally seeking out the secret sources of inspiration. Arrau knows how Beethoven felt when he composed the *Hammerklavier*. ("He was battling titanic conflicts in himself and reaching toward ecstasy.") He feels the loneliness of Brahms' late years that bore exquisite, bleak intermezzi, and he knows how Robert Schumann wrote his Fantasy in C as a love poem and won his woman and then, slowly, horribly, went insane, hearing the note A repeat in his brain, over and over and over, a klaxon from hell.

Musicologists know such things also, but not to the same piercing depth. Night after night, as he performs or practices majestic sonatas, Arrau experiences much of the composer's joy, the composer's torment. This gift, a kind of recreative genius, has made Arrau an emperor of the keyboard. He has been borne aloft by audiences in Moscow, called "positively humbling" by the *New York Times*, and achieved an enduring freshness. But being at one with great artists is not a quality acquired without suffering. "I could not have survived," Arrau said almost casually in the modest Vermont garden, "without forty years of psychoanalysis."

The real life of the virtuoso is rather different from what most of us imagine in our common hangover from the old classical-music movies. Flash. We see the virtuoso at the keys. Is that Cornel Wilde, coughing bravely as Chopin, or Dirk Bogarde pretending to be Liszt? Flash. Fingers dance on a mirrored keyboard and we hear eighteen bars of a concerto. Flash. Merle Oberon. Flash. Capucine. Flash. London, Paris, Rome. Flash. What a life.

The real virtuoso must exist between the dissolves. During a recent trip to Israel, Arrau enjoyed moments of adulation, but his bookings required him to play the *Emperor* Concerto seven times in the space of twelve days. "It is not, I imagine, like work on an assembly line," he says, "but repetition threatens the unprepared or immature artist with ennui. He is only playing the same notes night after night."

The parallel threat is a fear of waning powers. The virtuoso forever runs races against himself, matching or, ideally, surpassing his last performance. Around him critics bray. Too slow. Too mannered. Too fast. And tireless time assaults the fingers. Can he perform as well tonight as he did in Los Angeles last week? In Vienna last year? In Carnegie Hall ten years ago? Musicians collapse under such pressure. Hypochondria thrives. Tantrums prevail. Premature retirement, nervous breakdown, even suicide are the dark endings certain virtuosi find.

"The solution," Arrau says, "is to go beyond the notes, above the critics and reach toward Beethoven's soul. Beethoven's depths stir other depths within myself. But that in itself can be terrifying, like reaching toward a demanding god. It is too much for anyone to handle by himself. In my ideal musical school, not only harmony but psychoanalysis would be a mandatory part of the curriculum."

Giving a great concert, Arrau believes, "is a kind of miracle, but the miracle can only happen when the artist is 200 percent prepared to make it happen. And sometimes, one simply is not. The consequences, even in the best of mental health, can be quite shattering."

Early in the summer of 1972, Arrau planned an ambitious Monday night concert program for Royal Festival Hall—three solo works and two concerti accompanied by the London Philharmonic. When he flew into London on a Saturday, he was sneezing.

"A psychosomatic cold, maestro?" asked Friede Rothe, one of his managers.

"Probably," Arrau said, lightly. His face was grave.

The rehearsal Monday morning was accurate, but wanted fire. "It won't go," Arrau said. Then he rode back to his hotel and went to sleep.

Ian Hunter, his British representative, and Miss Rothe sent for a physician, who found nothing seriously wrong. At 3:30 in the afternoon, when Arrau ritually reviews the scores that he will play, he had gone back to sleep. Now Hunter and Miss Rothe realized that truly he might cancel, losing his own fee— sometimes as high as $8,000—and costing the impresarios $15,-000 in refunds.

Arrau woke near five. "I'm not playing," he said. "I'm sorry, they will have to give back the money." His face blackened and took on a look of utmost misery, which presently became his normal expression. For days he would not approach a piano. He lost his temper during an inconsequential disagreement about a popular novel, *The Godfather.* He seemed suddenly smaller, older, infinitely weary.

He canceled another performance and then, six bleak days later, tramped to the Steinway at five o'clock in the afternoon and began to practice a Chopin concerto. His playing was fiery, almost violent, with pent-up intensity, and he would not leave the piano bench for five hours. "I am fine," he said at 10 P.M. He resumed concertizing the next night.

No one can explain all the sources of such incidents. Certainly Arrau was suffering from a fatigue of the spirit. Perhaps his mind, wanting to restore itself, put up a psychic rebellion. But for how long would this go on? How could he combat knifing fears that this might be a sudden onset of aridity? Was this the end of Claudio Arrau, virtuoso?

Arrau and I met in 1970, the two-hundredth anniversary of the birth of his demanding god, Beethoven. Arrau celebrated by beginning a new edition of the piano sonatas, and by performing them in one hundred concerts in seventy major cities from Rio to Tokyo. At Lincoln Center in late autumn Arrau played the three last sonatas, music that possesses mysterious qualities, a mix of peace and ecstasy that Beethoven was able to realize after twenty years of deafness. There is no more difficult music for the piano, no work that demands so much of the pianist's spirit. When Beethoven composed them, Arrau believes, "he broke the bonds of time and must have felt like Jonah coming out of the whale, man's oldest symbolic story of the journey from darkness to light."

That cold November night, Arrau's performances spun a profound and not quite definable effect on a blasé subscription audience. Some concerts make you want to cheer with excitement. Some can draw tears. Listening to Arrau's late Beethoven was rousing at times, poignant at others, but in the end something more than either. Listening, I felt myself being led into new chambers of consciousness—my own consciousness, Arrau's, Beethoven's.

Then, so as not to conclude on too intimate a chord, Arrau gave a bravura performance of the *Appassionata,* a heroic work out of Beethoven's thirties. The audience stood up and shouted then and Arrau had to take eight curtain calls.

Backstage I found a small man, not more than five foot six, his collar wet and the flesh of his face drooping with fatigue. He was thanking someone in German, someone else in Spanish.

"I've never heard such trills as you played in Opus 111," I said.

"Yes," Arrau said, through exhaustion. "Yes? You are too kind."

Toward spring, Arrau invited me to observe a master class at his home in Douglaston, Long Island. There he would consciously be translating his musical approach into words. It is a comfortable white stone house, overlooking a bay, but undistinguished from the outside, the sort of house where one might find an internist raising four children and dabbling with photography on Sundays and Wednesday afternoons. But inside, in a soft blend of paneled rooms, you find a wonder of pre-Columbian figurines, Renaissance portraits and bookcases bearing Schiller in German, Cervantes in Spanish, Styron in English.

A flight of stairs leads down to the music room, a spacious rectangle with a stone fireplace. On one table stands a stereo phonograph, which Arrau has never learned to operate. He cannot drive a car either. The walls are covered with paintings collected on concert tours. One Madonna, painted on wood, dates from the fourteenth century. Statuettes are everywhere, and a stone from Masada, the last fortress of the ancient Hebrew warriors, a candelabrum from Florence, and exquisite Benin bronzes from Africa. But what dominates the room, standing in an airy corner, is the grand piano, *Arrau's* grand piano.

About a score of invited guests—musicians, advanced students, teachers—milled in the room. Their talk stilled as Arrau appeared, wearing a black high-necked tunic, on which white buttons sparkled. He was smiling. Chairs were placed in rows. Arrau alone sat behind the keyboard. There a young Brazilian pianist, who was going to perform the first movement of Brahms' Second Concerto, grimaced nervously. At a slight nod from Arrau, the Brazilian sounded the first regal chords. Arrau's face twisted in concentration.

"No, no," he would say quietly, "too harsh." Or, "Remember the diminuendo goes softer only, not slower." Or, "Here the melody the orchestra plays is a garland. You must weave a bouquet about it. You must play delicately with a most fluid tone."

Arrau extended his own elbows and made a graceful flapping movement with his arms. "Loosen the shoulders. To have the fluid tone for pianissimo, you must keep your body fluid, the muscles, the arms, the shoulders fluid."

Arrau leaned forward and I wondered if he would play the passage himself—hoped more than wondered—but then he sat back very rigidly, hands stiff before him, imitating the posture of certain Russian-trained pianists. "Play like this in a strait jacket," he said, "and you will end in a strait jacket."

"I have missed some notes," the Brazilian said.

"I have heard. With practice you will stop making mistakes." Arrau and the young man worked through the movement bar by bar.

"I never show a pupil by playing myself," Arrau said afterward, as we sipped drinks in a study.

"You would dazzle him?"

"He would try to play as I, try to copy, instead of reaching his own understanding."

"Maestro," someone said, "how was the Beethoven tour?"

"In Milano it was as if no one had seen each other for days. During one pianissimo, I could hear from all over the hall people calling to each other, '*Ciao, ciao.*' But in Prague, nineteen curtain calls."

Someone mentioned Russian composers. "Shostakovich," Arrau said, "has not written one good note of piano music. No. Let me correct that. He has written one good note, but not two. Rachmaninoff is for the movies."

"Yes," said Friede Rothe, "but the maestro once played Rachmaninoff for the score of a movie called *Rhapsody*, starring Elizabeth Taylor."

"One endures such moments to survive," Arrau said, with his faint, warm smile. Around him cocktail ice and conversation tinkled.

No one auditing the bright, postmusicale chatter would have suspected that the trim, gracious artist at its center had endured the collapse of three earlier careers, had battled obsessions with death and had waged the ceaseless struggle for realization that is the curse and the glory of an artist's life. By the time I came to the summer house in Vermont, I had seen Arrau many other times: small parties following recitals, a gathering to celebrate a South American tour. "I needed a police escort in Rio," he said, cheerfully, "like Frank Sinatra or the Beatles." He had talked about serious things lightly in the manner of cocktail parties and, also in the manner of cocktail parties, we had agreed that next time we would get below the surface.

Each year Arrau allows himself four summer weeks in Vermont, "to keep my head clear," he says. But he feels uneasy away from the thorny delights of a Steinway, so he was combining this vacation with a concert, one concert in a tiny theater at Manchester that would be a benefit for young musicians.

The day before he played at Manchester would be a welcome time to visit, Arrau suggested. He could be most open amid the willows and maples of his four hundred country acres.

As we approached the house from the garden, Arrau excused himself. He is a rather formal man, and he would be uncomfortable receiving one within while wearing work clothes. Other guests were shooed into the living room, and when Arrau returned, now in trim slacks and a sports shirt, he led me into the study of his retreat. It is sparer than the music room in Douglaston, but bright, with windows on three sides, pine furniture, New England antiques and the inevitable ebony Steinway. Stacks of notepaper lay on the piano. The fingering of one phrase in a Beethoven sonata troubled Arrau. He walked to the piano, stooped and played the passage three times with enormous power. The effect was breathtaking, a thundering statement, heard thrice over, in a little room.

Arrau shrugged, jotted briefly on the notepaper and settled into an armchair.

"I wanted to ask about your psychotherapy," I said.

"Why not begin at the beginning?" Arrau said. "My father—he was an oculist—died before I was one year old."

"Have you any memory of that? Do you remember coming to music?"

"My father, no. Indeed, I have looked many times for father symbols. But I cannot *not* remember music. In Chillán, where I was born, a Chilean town with no more than thirty thousand persons, my mother, Lucretia, gave piano lessons. I was the last child, born after twenty-one years of marriage. I remember quite clearly going to a piano, sixty-five years ago. I can see the black upright. Two candles stand on it. And the music. I read music as other children look at picture books. Sheets of music *became* my picture books.

"In my mind, some notes were insects. Others, linked by black lines, were avalanches. Still other notes were mountaineers tied together. The pause marking was an enormous eye staring out from under a fierce eyebrow." Arrau leaned back and placed a strong hand to his forehead. "And through some sublime process that no one yet understands I taught myself to read music by the time I was four. When I awoke, it seems, I was playing the piano."

At five, Arrau made his concert debut, playing Schumann and Mozart. Lucretia was frightened by Claudio's talent but determined. At six he played in Santiago, at seven in Buenos Aires, and at eight he was sent to Berlin with his mother and sister on a ten-year scholarship established by the Chilean Congress. Then he first brushed against despair.

"The first two teachers in Berlin were boring," Arrau said. "I wanted only to read more music, to perform more music. I was the child discovering *Märchenbilder*, a fairyland. Purposely, these teachers slowed me. They gave me endless exercises. At eight I loved the piano so, I would take my meals at the keyboard. By ten dull teaching had turned me against music and myself. Music bored me. To how many people does that befall, to how many prodigies?"

"But you were rescued."

"In a sense by Beethoven." Arrau's brown hair was brushed back. His mobile face lit. "Beethoven had a pupil named Czerny. Czerny taught Franz Liszt. And Liszt had taught a musician called Martin Krause.

"Desperate at ten, I was taken to play for Krause. He was a severe old man, but children feel reality and behind this harsh mask was an incredible gift for opening up worlds. When I finished my audition, Krause said, 'Give me a chance. I will bring you back to music.' Then he said to my mother, 'This child shall be my masterpiece.'"

Arrau paused and let slip a sigh. It was extraordinary how he brought back dead times in such detail, the first notes, the words, the crystal world of Berlin. "Krause was terribly demanding. He escorted me to museums, guided my reading, found other children with whom I could play. He taught me that an artist cannot be a great artist without interest in all the arts, in all of life. And he could show me how Liszt himself broke a chord." Arrau's long fingers rolled on the little table as he spoke.

The beginning piano student plays a chord, say the three notes of a C major triad, all at once with a sodden plunk. But Liszt discovered that chords could be struck with a rolling motion, the notes stroked a split second apart. "In innumerable ways," Arrau said. "Slowly with a crescendo toward the upper note. Fast with a diminuendo. Starting with a slow roll and becoming faster. Innumerable." From such subtleties spring great concerts.

Arrau, at twelve the spiritual grandchild of Liszt, became a descendant of Mozart, the infinite prodigy. "Krause and I traveled through Germany," Arrau said. "I played for the King of Saxony, the King of Bavaria, the ducal courts. And the kings and dukes showered me with gifts. I still have a necktie pin with the letter 'M' and a gorgeous crown of diamonds. That was given to me by Queen Marie of Rumania in 1913." The fairyland survived for only six years. In August 1918, Martin Krause contracted pneumonia. "He died in a month," Arrau said, "and now I was inconsolably alone."

Lucretia immediately suggested another teacher. "But *Krause* was my teacher," Arrau said. "Intuitively, I felt that anything a teacher could show me had been shown. The rest I would have to learn for myself. This firm decision was artisti- cally correct, but to live with it would have taken a superman and I was far from that. I was at adolescence, when you wake up in the middle of the night and say, 'Why did I do what I did?' Deterioration took hold of me like a disease. Things combined. The death. The time in my life.

"At first I made many mistakes. Then I could no longer play certain works. People repeated the fallacy people always repeat about a prodigy: 'He was only a *Wunderkind,* already spent.' In 1919 my career was gone for a second time and now I thought of, perhaps longed for, my own death."

One learns more of Arrau at this life crisis from the analyst he turned to for help. Dr. Hubert Abrahamsohn survived in Munich into his eighties, doing his own housekeeping, in a fifth- floor apartment in the Schwabing district, where writers and musicians live. Abrahamsohn had been studying under the Swiss master Dr. Carl Jung when Arrau came to him, despond- ent. "He was the center of very strong forces," Abrahamsohn recalled. "His mother never entered the room when Claudio was playing, but listened beyond to every note, and concen- trated the full force of an overpowering personality on him."

Abrahamsohn had large pale eyes and a huge head. In repose he reminded people of a Buddha. "I was, to be sure, learning many things myself, but quickly it was clear that Claudio looked on Krause as a father figure. For years he was blocked from performing certain music which in his mind was very close to

Krause's memory." Together long ago, the apprentice Jungian and the stymied, aging *Wunderkind* explored the life streams of creation.

The continuing process required a certain acceptance of conflict. "Some have suggested that Beethoven composed out of conflict, which is true," Arrau says, "and with a thorough analysis the conflict would be resolved and the creativity would vanish. But the good analyst, and Abrahamsohn was a very good analyst, has the sense to leave certain vital conflict alone and work to eliminate only what is destructive. That is a tricky business, to be sure."

In his Vermont study, Arrau recaptured the dialogues. "A prodigy," he said, leaning forward with great intensity, "has a divine unconscious innocence. He performs through a kind of joy. But the artist has a *conscious* responsibility—to himself, to Beethoven, to Liszt. Passing over from prodigy to man is an act of supreme heroism.

"No less than Ulysses, an artist undergoes trial after trial as he advances. He must play a sonata more profoundly, reach for deeper levels of fulfillment. That is what he does if all goes well, but most of the time all does not go well in life. Then the artist enacts an expression of what Jung defined as a period of self-destruction."

"Few jump from bridges," I said.

"But peculiar things happen," Arrau said. "We develop severe colds before important appearances. Singers come down with inexplicable cases of laryngitis. Instrumentalists lose the use of their fingers. We provoke scenes and walk out on waiting audiences. We are trying to give up the artist's life. When I was eighteen, I was willing to, longed to, believe that the artist in me was dead."

The treatment was nothing less than an extended confrontation with the soul. "I had to clear away a psychic jungle," Arrau said. "With Abrahamsohn, layer after layer of covering was stripped away. My mother's ambitions for me were intense. She expected divinity from her son. So did Martin Krause, who was really my second father." Arrau arose and began to pace. "Slowly, I was brought to realize a terrible weakness in myself. Vanity. I was playing for my own glory. But I am not divine nor even a creative artist. I am a *recreative* artist. My highest purpose is to bear to you not my spirit but the spirit of the composer. Can you understand how difficult that was to accept?"

"I think so," I said.

"Well, we both know famous musicians who have not been able to accept that in seventy years," Arrau said.

During his twenties in Berlin, Arrau supported himself by giving piano lessons and began to remake his career. Europe was crowded with renowned pianists, and Arrau with his introspective style moved toward prominence very slowly. Then, in 1935, following two harrowing years of concentration, he performed all of Bach's keyboard music in a series of twelve recitals. No musician had done that before. "It began as a trick," Arrau said, "a conscious effort to call attention to my career. Critics were awed by my memory, and I had discovered something. I made the same experiment, all the Mozart in five concerts, all the Schumann, all the Liszt. What I discovered was that by knowing *all* a composer's output, you can understand *each* work better. You grasp relationships, the whole creative life. You grow yourself."

By now Arrau was breaking free of the old shackles. In 1938 he married Ruth Schneider, an attractive soprano from Frankfurt. His concerts were becoming a rage in Europe. But then the black tide of the Nazis drove him to America and he had to make a fresh career all over again.

"You cannot imagine the devastation of Hitler," Arrau said in the cool Vermont study. Outside it had begun to shower and you could hear raindrops splatter on the leaves. "We had in

Berlin the center of the world and the fool from Berchtesgaden came in and in a few months we had a provincial town. We lost Schnabel and Bruno Walter and Rudolf Serkin and Otto Klemperer.

"And myself, I thought it would not last. How could it last? It was too foolish, too ridiculous, too stupid, and here were my final years in Germany, my private revival, my victory, coinciding with the triumph of a madman." Arrau shook his head. "Ach," he said. "But at least I was able to help some Jewish musicians to escape."

His American successes came slowly through his forties and fifties. Some critics found his work affected. He himself says, "I was again going through crises." Sometimes, it seemed, he put too much of himself in a work; sometimes too little. Children were born. Mario runs a dude ranch next to the Vermont estate. Carmen is a housewife living in Washington. Chris, growing up in Douglaston, is preoccupied with the New York Mets.

"Was there a point," I said, "when you felt your artistry became complete?"

"It still evolves," Arrau said, "but in the 1950s, here and in London and everywhere, the acclaim became very great. Now in the 1970s, I play with more joy and abandon and confidence and discipline than I have ever before."

"Your psychoanalysis is finished?"

"Yes, although sometimes so much goes on about my head I have to cancel. Now that is rare."

"But playing the same music over and over," I said. "Doesn't one get weary of the same sonata?"

"Does one get tired of the beating of the heart?" Arrau said. "Because that is what great music is—the beating of an anguished, battling, triumphant, transcendent heart."

The next night he played Liszt's Sonata in a small pavilion at Manchester, Vermont. The work is beautiful and pained, with singing melodies in the treble that contend with a growling agitated bass. Arrau's performance was a wonder. The left hand brought forth ominous dissonance and the treble choired love songs, and as he reigned over the conflict at the piano his body twisted and his face contorted and in the still, rainy Vermont night performer and composer and music were one.

Afterward Arrau scuttled happily about the living room in the summer house. "I *was* the conveyer." he said, "It was Liszt you heard." There could be some improvements perhaps later, he thought. But it had been a nice beginning. Now charged with an unfettered energy, Claudio Arrau rubbed his hands and ordered special brandy, and though seventy was beckoning, he beamed like a youngster at the challenge and glory of the concert season ahead.

III
Police Blotter

*The essential power to pursue
relentlessly; the special privilege
to riot and go free.*

The Case
of the Butchered
Bookmaker

That section of Brooklyn endowed with the gracious colonial name of Williamsburg is a warren of synagogues, cut-rate stores and neglected tenements. Now Puerto Ricans and public housing are coming to Williamsburg, but for a long time the neighborhood belonged to Jews without money.

There was a roiling sameness to the old Jewish ghettos of New York. The people had come from Eastern Europe after waves of Polish pogroms, and though they were free here and safe, they clung to their old ways. Everywhere streets with decidedly nonghetto names—Moore, Delancey, Hopkinson—became loud with the nasal, fluting rhythms of Polish Yiddish.

Unschooled in English, initially unsure of America, immigrant men who were learned in Talmudic law stayed in their ghettos and went to work as pants pressers, butchers and peddlers. Suspicion, like terror, was part of the ghetto tradition. Someday, tradition told these immigrants, the Christian outsider, the goy, would invade the ghetto and make trouble, just as goyim had made trouble in Spain, in Greece, in the Ukraine. There were Jews living among goyim here in America, but those Jews were themselves outsiders. Trust no outsider, tradition proclaimed. Follow the rabbit's defense. Learn to hide. The other—the only other—defense that ghetto Jews conceived was to develop a *Yiddische kopf,* a Jewish head, intelligence.

Peddlers and butchers drove their sons to music lessons, to libraries, to the great, free learning institutions of New York, seeking education as a shield. The results were altogether different from anything in the ghetto tradition. One was the decline of ghettos themselves, as second-generation Jews found that they could trust the American community, and the American community found that it could trust Jews. Another was the explosion of gifted, ambitious and suddenly emancipated people. George Gershwin and Paul Muni burst from a Manhattan ghetto called the Lower East Side. John Garfield and Danny Kaye burst from a Brooklyn ghetto called Brownsville. Out of these neighborhoods came professors, physicists, historians, linguists, educators.

By comparison, Williamsburg lagged. No one knows why, but instead of producing contemporary men, Williamsburg attracted a Jewish sect called Hasidim, whose members are fanatically devoted to the past and whose leaders sport the costumes of eighteenth-century Polish ghettos. In Williamsburg, intellectuality did not seem to be the end of men's ambition. The aim was shrewdness. Rather than nurture professors of philosophy, Williamsburg developed local renown as the spawning ground of bookmakers, basketball fixers and ticket scalpers, a quick-witted unattractive rabble. Outsiders were not merely distrusted. They were, whenever possible, fleeced.

One of the newest generation of Williamsburg bookmakers, a low-pressure lawbreaker named Rubin Markowitz, was murdered early in the 1960s while trying to collect from a client who was an outsider. They are still furious about that in Williamsburg. They think that plugging a bookie violates most of the Ten Commandments, and they may be even more upset that one of their boys let himself get so badly outmaneuvered. They were fully prepared to hire an assassin if the District Attorney failed to convict Rubin Markowitz's murderer. "Where," asks a citizen of Williamsburg, "did that rat come off shooting Ruby? Believe me, Ruby was one terrific guy. I'll tell you how terrific, if you make it worth my while. I mean, how much will you pay for me to tell you about my dead friend who was a real great guy?"

According to testimony at the trial in New York, a business-man from Park Avenue shot the bookie. The businessman, Mark Fein, did not testify and was convicted of second-degree murder.

Once he lived in a $65,000 cooperative duplex, with three children, a stylish wife and a nurse. He drove a white Lincoln Continental and had his suits custom-made. Mark Fein liked to display the trappings of wealth, and it is true that his father, Irving Fein, founder of a tin-can company, is a multimillionaire. But Mark Fein, a man of various vices, apparently was not comfortable sharing problems with his father. Nor was he able to draw on his father's bank accounts. On the surface the two were cordial and hearty. Beneath there seemed to be the kind of blankness that precluded discussion of anything more mean-ingful than how to play a hand at gin rummy. The aggressively wealthy father and the morally stunted son remained remote until Mark was arrested. Then, too late, they embraced each other and sobbed.

The smallest of Mark Fein's vices was a compulsive urge to gamble, slightly beyond his own means, which were consider-able. Probably, going beyond one's means is the only real gam-bling. There is a theory that if a man can afford to lose a bet, he is playing a game, but he is not gambling. Real gambling denotes, as consequences of losing, real anguish, real hardship.

Nongambling connoisseurs remember the 1963 World Series as the one in which Sandy Koufax, the fastest left-hander who ever graduated from Lafayette High School in Brooklyn, over-powered the New York Yankees. Working for the Los Angeles

Dodgers, Koufax established a strike-out record in winning the first game and concluded the only Dodger Series sweep in recorded history by winning the fourth. Mark Fein, who once attended but did not graduate from Lafayette High, remembers that Series as a disaster. He bet the Yankees steadily and heavily. When Koufax was through, Fein owed Rubin Markowitz, the bookmaker, $7,200. Two of Fein's intimates and associates had followed the Fein line. They owed Markowitz an additional $16,690. The total of $23,890 was the biggest potential payoff in Markowitz's career, and if there was one man more cheerful than Sandy Koufax when the 1963 Series ended, it was Rubin Markowitz. "I'm going to use the dough to get into something legit," he repeated hysterically, "like maybe a concession at the next World's Fair."

A difficulty for everyone, bettors and bookie alike, was that Fein and his friends had lost more money than they could conveniently raise. His two friends turned to Mark Fein, who liked to boast about his means and his credit at New York banks. Fein assured them that he would settle with the bookmaker. There could be a final accounting among the three friends later. "No sweat," Mark Fein said.

Fein, according to prosecution witnesses, settled with Markowitz in the dinette of a bachelor apartment he maintained under another name. There, at 406 East Sixty-third Street in Manhattan, he shot the bookmaker twice in the chest, knocking him from a chair. "Oh, my God," Rubin Markowitz shrieked from the floor, and Fein emptied the pistol at his face. Then Fein bound Rubin Markowitz, who was now a corpse, with clothesline and stuffed the body into a large, cheap trunk he had purchased in Spanish Harlem.

To dispose of the body, Fein telephoned his mistress, a thirty-seven-year-old prostitute and madam, who changed her name once or twice a year, as casually as other women have their teeth examined. When Fein telephoned his mistress, she was calling herself Gloria Kendal. She was also, at the moment, preparing to leave for a course she had been taking at the Swedish Institute School for Massage. Like an old baseball player, Miss Kendal at thirty-seven was investigating fresh fields for the future.

As a witness, Gloria recalled the dialogue of that night:

"I'd like to see you," Mark Fein said.

"That's impossible," Gloria said. "You'll have to wait until I finish school."

"Gloria," Fein said, "I can't wait. I have to see you right away."

Gloria Kendal understood men's bursts of need. "I *have* to go to school," she said, "but can I send somebody else over to take care of you?"

"Please, Gloria, I must see *you*," Fein said. "Don't fail me."

Gloria took a taxi. Fein was flushed and keyed up when she entered the apartment. In the living room stood the trunk. "What happened here?" Gloria asked.

"I'll bet you can't tell me what's inside the trunk," Fein said. As a detective later noted, he was still betting.

"I have no idea," Gloria said, somewhat irritated by this disruption of her day.

"It's the body of a dead man, my bookmaker, Ruby," Fein said, according to Gloria's testimony. "I had to meet him this afternoon to pay him. And I met him at four o'clock. And he came up here. And we were talking. And we had words. And I shot him."

Gloria stood her ground. She did not faint or scream or gasp, and Fein became more confident. He had really killed the bookie for a friend who was broke, he said. But shock was assaulting Gloria, and she was silent. "Please help me," Mark Fein cried out. "There's nobody else I can turn to. I can't call my friends or my family. You're the only one. Please."

With a small sigh, Gloria said, "What do you want me to do?"

Fein's poise returned. "Help me get the trunk out of here and get rid of it," he said.

Gloria made a brief, weak attempt at getting no further involved. "Why don't you call the police?" she said. "Tell them that while you were talking to this man, somebody came in and shot him, stole the money and ran out."

This was inept for a woman who had spent years lying to cops; it would even have been inept for a television writer. The evidence is that Gloria was in deeper shock than she realized.

"That's good," she remembers Fein saying pleasantly across Rubin Markowitz's corpse, "but I can't be involved with the police. I'd be ruined socially and financially if I was involved with the police or a bookmaker." Fein then told Gloria to call a friend because the trunk "is heavy."

Gloria telephoned an unemployed hairdresser in the Bronx named David Broudy, with the news that she had found him work. She skipped the details, and when Broudy reached the apartment and saw the trunk, he asked, "What's in there? A body?"

"You guessed it," Gloria said.

A curious young lady named Geraldine Boxer had been planning to drive Gloria to the Swedish Institute School for Massage. Following messages, Miss Boxer showed up at the apartment, too. Thus there was one corpse, one killer and three possible accessories, any one of whom might at any time have raced into the hallway crying murder. To ease anxieties, Mark Fein served vodka.

Once you accept an absurd premise you are, for good or ill, quite lost. Give a playwright an absurd premise and you are lost in fantasy. Give a politician an absurd premise and you are lost in a windstorm. Give Mark Fein the absurd premise that it is your obligation to help him get away with murder and you are caught in the kind of conversation that took place in apartment 5B at 406 East Sixty-third Street about sunset on October 10, 1963.

Everyone who was there gave Fein his premise simply by remaining. Miss Kendal testified that she briefly saw the corpse. David Broudy told the jury he knew it existed. Miss Boxer insists that she thought the trunk contained tax records. Simply by momentum, once these people elected to stay with Mark Fein and drink his vodka, they had to worry with him, work for him and help him. That, as Kendal, Broudy and Boxer testified, left the business of details:

Obviously, the place for the trunk was a river, just like in the old movies. But, David Broudy pointed out, the object in the trunk was not chopped liver. Would the trunk leak? He wanted to know.

"No," Fein said. It had been hard work, but he had lined the trunk well.

"Whose car?" Gloria wondered. Fein ruled out his Lincoln— too dangerous. Miss Boxer's car was too small. David's?

"Oh, no," David Broudy said. "Nobody's moving that thing in my heap."

"I'll rent a station wagon," Fein said.

Leaving apartment, trunk and corpse to Broudy and Miss Boxer, Mark Fein and Gloria Kendal took a taxi to a garage and rented a beige wagon. "Put the wagon on my charge," Fein told the attendant.

Driving back to the apartment, Fein mentioned an additional problem. "Gee, Gloria, I promised my wife I'd take her to dinner."

"All right, Mark," Gloria said, relieved to find at last a familiar situation. "You go home and pull yourself together. We'll take care of everything, as soon as you and David load the trunk." Fein double-parked the beige wagon outside 406 East Sixty-third Street, risking a ticket.

Even though the building has an elevator, Broudy said he and Fein had a hard time with the corpse in the trunk. Ruby Markowitz's body weighed almost two hundred pounds. Finally, sweaty in the street, Fein said to Broudy, "I really want to thank you for helping me out." The trunk fitted easily in the rear of the wagon. "I'll see you around," Mark Fein added, and walked off toward his white Lincoln.

As the three testified at the trial, Broudy drove the station wagon, with Gloria Kendal and Geri Boxer alongside him in the front seat. They cruised a few blocks to an entrance onto the Franklin D. Roosevelt Drive, which runs along the eastern rim of Manhattan. David saw a break in traffic and pulled close to the East River. Suddenly police cars lit the night with flashing blinkers. (A rabid dog had been reported nearby.) David drove on. He did not stop again until he had reached 179th Street, past the East River alongside of the Harlem River, which forms a northern border of Manhattan. Quickly, Broudy, Miss Kendal and Miss Boxer hoisted the trunk over the Harlem River sea wall. They heard a bump, as though the huge trunk had struck a rock outcropping, and then a splash. No cars had passed. No one had seen them.

Mostly in silence, they drove downtown to Madison Square Garden, so that Gloria could buy tickets to a forthcoming performance of the Bolshoi Ballet. Then they went to a medium-priced French restaurant, where Gloria ordered wine and lent Broudy money to pay the check.

At about the time Markowitz's corpse plunged through the cold and oily Harlem River, Fein was taking a hot shower in his Park Avenue duplex. He had promised his wife dinner, and he was a man of his word. With her he returned to East Sixty-third Street, in bravado or indifference, this time to No. 26, which housed a restaurant called Quo Vadis—"Whither Goest Thou?" There Mr. and Mrs. Mark Fein ate well.

One is inclined to conclude that Fein returned to Sixty-third Street in indifference, because beyond anything else the murder was an act of contempt. Like all murders it was brutal, cruel, foul, but the special quality of this murder was that the man who had moved to Park Avenue slew the man who came from Williamsburg as anyone else might swat a large, persistent insect. When he fired his .22-caliber pistol, Mark Fein seemed to be demanding: "Who are you, grubby ghetto Jew, to bother someone like me?" It was an uncomplicated message, and the bookie from the ghetto, two bullets in his chest, finding The Outsider where he had expected none, could only scream, "Oh, my God!"

By any standard, including police as well as Williamsburg standards, Mark Fein appeared to be an absurd candidate for killer. He is bespectacled, mild-mannered, and, before going to prison, he was natty. He seemed to want recognition inordinately, and he would become indignant when headwaiters failed to offer him a prime table. He was arrogant about his family's wealth, and once he shouted at a minor bank official who refused to cash his check. Mostly, he was timid. Even his rages seemed small.

Fein's I.Q. is average (108), but he was a below-average student. His father, a driving and driven man, shipped him from Lafayette High to a military school in Georgia, which must have seemed a severe rejection. Mark was back home in a year, still a poor student, to attend a private academy in Brooklyn. Finally, he quit altogether, without a diploma. This was unfortunate, but hardly unique among young men who have a family business waiting, whatever may befall them in intermediate algebra.

Subsequently, life eased considerably for Mark Fein. Under his father's direction he did nicely in the tin-can business, meeting buyers, arranging deals, closing sales. In 1956 he made what appeared to be an excellent marriage. Nancy Nahon, a dark-haired and attractive bride, also came from a family of means. Friends called her "lively," "winning," and if she was "on the make for the good life," she was also "bright."

Irving Fein, pleased with his son's marriage, soon occupied himself with other matters. His tin-can company was prosperous, but prosperity apparently was not enough for Irving Fein. He wanted a fortune. After extensive and complicated negotiations he sold his business to a larger firm called the U.S. Hoffman Machinery Corporation. The selling price has been estimated at $10 million and, as Irving Fein knew, a corporate sale is capital gain, not income. The tax rate on a capital gain never exceeded 25 percent at that time. A man who made $10 million may have gotten to keep as much as $7.5 million.

Out of tin cans, rich Irving Fein installed himself in the business of selling corrugated boxes, an allied field. He was comfortable in the box business and it, too, went well. His personal fortune secure, his new business thriving, Irving Fein eased himself back to chairman of the board. He proudly announced that his successor as president would be Mark.

When Mark Fein moved to Park Avenue, four years before the murder of Rubin Markowitz, he was twenty-eight years old and he already possessed wealth, position and a handsome wife. It was logical to assume that he could afford to pay his bookie. It was logical to assume that if he needed money badly, he could turn to his father, the millionaire. It was logical to assume that if, for some unaccountable reason, he had been involved in the murder of Markowitz, someone else had done the actual killing. Mark Fein, however, lived without logic. He was flawed. It was as if a portion of his being had never developed, or did not exist. Broadly, that portion coincides with civilization.

October 11, 1963, is the day the story begins in police records. That evening a woman named Naomi Markowitz went to a Brooklyn police station to report that her husband, Ruby, was missing. Her husband, Mrs. Markowitz explained, was a good man and a dependable provider. He took home $90 a week as a grocery clerk at the J & H Food Center in Williamsburg, and out of that, Mrs. Markowitz said, he always turned over $70 to her. The police station was in Sheepshead Bay, a neighborhood of faceless new apartment buildings where, when the wind is right, you can catch a scent of the Atlantic Ocean. She and Ruby had two lovely children, Mrs. Markowitz told the police, and it was for them that Ruby had moved to Sheepshead Bay from Williamsburg. He never missed a night at home, she said. He was never even late. He was a regular nut about promptness.

That was why, Naomi Markowitz said, she was so afraid that something had happened to him.

Naomi Markowitz's recitation was incomplete, but it is a measure of the panic rampant among the family, friends and associates of Rubin Markowitz that anyone went to the police at all. To gambling people from Williamsburg, frank talk to cops is lunacy. So, even in their desperation, the people from Williamsburg decided not to give in completely. They would talk to the police, but not frankly.

Tradition and recent memory influenced their thinking. Tradition proclaimed that cops were dangerous outsiders. Besides, within the last twenty years, during the mayoralty of the late William O'Dwyer, a Brooklyn gambling man named Harry Gross had bought himself a small army of policemen, only to have unapproached cops send him to jail. This proved, Williamsburg gambling men believe, that cops are crooks, looking for bribes, shakedowns, sellouts, and disloyal.

Unlike the Mafia, this generation of Williamsburg bookies is disinclined toward violence. For the most part they aspire toward coarse respectability, complete with mink capes on hot autumn nights and nephews taking the wrong courses at inferior colleges. "There ain't no percentage in violence," they say. "It don't figure any more. It's just for the dumb *Ee-talyani.*"

Before going to the police (lunacy), or considering violence (dumb), the Williamsburg people close to Ruby Markowitz had launched an investigation of their own. It was led by Jack Josephy, a shrewd, full-faced man who admits to having been in an odd partnership with Markowitz.

Josephy owns the J & H Food Center, where Ruby sometimes clerked. Beyond offering honest work, Josephy testified, he underwrote Ruby's bookmaking losses. Josephy insisted that he shared in losses only. "No profits," as any gambling man might protest to the Internal Revenue Service.

At 4 P.M., on the last day of his life, Ruby was to meet Fein in Manhattan on First Avenue in the sixties. After collecting

$23,890 he was to be at the corner of Madison Avenue and Thirty-second Street at 4:30. There he would pay a successful World Series bettor named Jerry (the Whale) Bergman $4,810. Then, $19,080 ahead, Ruby Markowitz would return to Brooklyn.

On October 10, Jerry the Whale was nervous. It was a mild, clear afternoon, 59 degrees when he started waiting, and a soft breeze blew from the southeast. Jerry the Whale perspired easily. He had been a bookmaker once himself, but two arrests did his nerves no good, and now he had found work as a shipping clerk.

The Whale sweated as he watched traffic clog Madison Avenue for half an hour. Then, at five, he telephoned Jack Josephy in the J & H Food Center to report that Ruby was late. "I'm gonna call around," Josephy said. "Keep checking me every half-hour till I find him." The Whale agreed and began wedging his three hundred pounds into telephone booths at thirty-minute intervals. At eight o'clock, he and Josephy drove through Manhattan streets in an aimless and unrewarding search.

A day later, Josephy spotted Markowitz's car parked on First Avenue near Sixty-fourth Street. In sudden, uncharacteristic panic, he went to a precinct house and asked a detective to examine it. "I was scared I'd find Ruby's body in the trunk," he testified in court. A detective examined the car, but found no body and no blood. "There's nothing here," he told Josephy. "You may as well take the car and go home." Late that evening Naomi Markowitz first reported that her husband, the grocery clerk, was missing.

Conning the cops would not work forever, Josephy realized. But there was always a chance Ruby might show up, and it didn't figure to reveal a hand too soon. Already some of the Williamsburg people spoke of sending out a contract to avenge Ruby. It was two days after Naomi Markowitz made her guarded statement that Jack Josephy led a shrill raggle-taggle group, including Jerry the Whale, into the Sheepshead Bay police station. Abruptly and honestly, Josephy talked in terms of thousands of dollars. Jerry the Whale, nervous in the presence of so many policemen, perspired heavily. The Brooklyn detectives were amused. Still, this was the occasion when police first heard the name of Mark Fein in connection with Rubin Markowitz.

Dutifully, they promised Josephy that they would investigate, even though, they told him, his friend would probably be around in a day or so, maybe without all the money. Josephy produced a picture of Markowitz and described his clothing. "Okay, okay," detectives told the Williamsburg people. "We'll see what we can do."

On October 15, five days after the murder, a Brooklyn detective named Eugene O'Neill called on Mark Fein at his office. In major investigations detectives interrogate in pairs so that there are two police witnesses to everything that takes place. Police regarded this interrogation as mere routine.

"Do you know a man named Rubin Markowitz?" O'Neill asked.

Behind black-rimmed spectacles, Mark Fein looked blank. Detective O'Neill showed Fein the picture.

"Oh, you must mean *Ruby* Markowitz," Fein said. "Yes, I know him."

"What are your business relationships with him?"

"I get theater and football tickets from him."

"Do you know Ruby as a bookmaker?" Detective O'Neill asked.

"No," Fein said.

"Do you ever bet with him?"

"No. I only get tickets from him."

"Did you see Markowitz on October 10?"

"No."

A few days later Fein went to see Detective O'Neill. This time Fein brought a lawyer. He had not been completely frank,

Fein said, because he had not wanted to get involved. He did indeed bet with Ruby Markowitz. So did some of his friends. At 3:30 or 3:45 on the afternoon of October 10 he had met Ruby on First Avenue "somewhere in the sixties" and paid off $23,890 in World Series betting losses. Someone else had been in the car with bookie Rubin Markowitz. The man was "about 45 years old, a white man with a dark complexion, wearing a gray suit and a fedora. He needed a shave and looked, uh, possibly Italian."

Despite the cliché description of a man from the Mafia, the story sounded plausible. It was perfectly plausible for a prosperous businessman to dodge getting involved in a search for a missing bookmaker. It was almost as plausible that a man from the Mafia had been in the car with Markowitz. Broke bookies borrow from Mafia sources, and hoodlums are not above muscling in on big gambling successes. Police eventually wasted weeks searching for a man in a gray fedora who looked, uh, possibly Italian.

Yet for all this the revised story which Fein, with legal advice, spun out to Detective O'Neill helped it doom its inventor. Beyond its seeming plausibility, *the story established Mark Fein as the last man who had seen Rubin Markowitz alive.* That was why police went back at him again and again.

His blunders would not have affected Mark Fein's future if Rubin Markowitz had remained a missing person. Theories of equal justice read nicely in police manuals, but detectives are not likely to investigate the disappearance of a bookmaker as thoroughly as they investigate the disappearance of a bank president. If one bookmaker had skipped town with illicit money, was New York City the poorer?

On the bleak, rainy morning of November 8, Ruby Markowitz ceased to be missing. At 6:10 that dawn a short, gruff drawbridge attendant named Fred Petrarca stared out through the downpour and, as he testified, "seen this big object inside the cribbing of the breakwater there." By noon police knew that four bullets had killed the big object. By midafternoon they had identified it as the disfigured remnant of Rubin Markowitz. The missing person had been found murdered, and the police investigation would now be of a different order. "Murder," Homicide Detective Frank Lyons, who cracked the case, points out with disarming cheer, "is something we treat a little different from running a stop sign."

Petrarca's drawbridge joins Manhattan Island to the Bronx over an angry stretch of estuary called Spuyten Duyvil, which is Dutch for "spitting devil." There the Harlem and Hudson rivers join in a boil of currents. Black-haired, intense Frank Lyons remembers driving to Spuyten Duyvil in the rain, considering glumly the prospect of having to view "a floater."

Prolonged immersion does dreadful things to the human body. Features swell horribly. Green lichens and water worms invade the flesh. Shrinking tendons constrict the face into a scream. The mass that was a man turns waxen, and chunks begin to fall away. Then there is the matter of odor.

The object that had been Rubin Markowitz was in water long enough to have bare bones showing for a nose, but not so long that one could forget this had been a man, who laughed and wept and who at his end cried out in agony and terror. "They ought to publish photographs of floaters," Lyons says in cold anger. "Then people would know the face of murder."

In the Manhattan morgue, the remnant was X-rayed. Four bullets appeared on the plates. As the skin dried and constricted, bullet holes became evident. Two were in the left side of the chest. The others were in the face, close to the chin.

Rubin Markowitz's pockets had not been emptied before his body was shoved into the trunk. Police found $441 in the pants, plus an address book and a variety of business cards. Technicians in a police laboratory dried the address book and the cards within hours after Fred Petrarca saw his big object in the rain. The first card that became legible was that of a ticket broker. "Good Lord," the broker cried to Detective Lyons, who had quickly called him, "that must be the body of Ruby Markowitz." By nightfall on November 8 police decided to release a story which the *Daily News* gaily headlined: "CLERK JEKYLL & BOOKIE HYDE FOUND SLAIN IN 24G PUZZLER." The *News* reported that the widow was astonished that her husband the grocery clerk had been found carrying $441. But higher in the article the *News* described Markowitz as "a good wireroom man with good clients." The paper added: "Authorities said his death occurred not long after he collected a $24,000 gambling debt from Mark Fein of 1095 Park Avenue, an executive of Fein Industries of 100 Park Avenue, box manufacturers."

Gloria Kendal, the prostitute, is not much of a newspaper reader. She tries, she says, to keep up with opera and ballet, but sometimes she is so busy there simply is no time for reading. She missed the *Daily News* of November 9, 1963. It was a few days later that David Broudy showed her the story. Gloria was utterly amazed. She testified that she telephoned Mark Fein. "What's the matter with you?" she asked. "Don't you look at TV? Haven't you ever heard of cement?"

Police concede that, if Markowitz's body had been properly disposed of, Fein might not have gone to prison. It is a simple matter of progression. No body, no proof of homicide. No homicide, no Detective Lyons, and his relentless painstaking investigation. No relentless investigation, no indictment, much less a conviction. It is remarkable that there was ever an indictment even after murder was established. "Everybody," Lyons said later, "told me Fein was sure to get away."

In November, Lyons had on his hands not much more than a corpse, spoken for by a variety of Williamsburg gamblers. "I'm leveling with you, Detective," people insisted. "Ruby didn't go to no loan sharks for money. He didn't know no mob guys. We ain't that kinda people. A little bookmaking, hah, you understand? But you make a bet yourself, hah, Detective? It's a sin a man should make a bet?" Looking for loan sharks and Mafia figures in the life of Ruby Markowitz was to occupy Detective

Lyons for months. There are few chores harder—and generally duller—than looking for persons who do not exist.

Meanwhile, there was the unpromising matter of Mark Fein to check out. Fein was now the last person who admitted seeing not a missing man but a murder victim alive. Still, in those first days after the remnant of Markowitz appeared, Fein was not a very imposing suspect. He seemed too rich, too timid, too soft.

But Detective Frank Lyons, homicide expert, son of a homicide expert, descendant of Ireland and a Catholic, heard something that impressed him in the ghetto-scarred speech of the Williamsburg people. It is not something he can classify precisely, but it has to do with rhythms and intonations of speech. "A lie," Detective Lyons says, "is out of rhythm. It's something that somehow, if you have trained yourself, you can pick up. With the truth, the rhythm stays true." Nothing significant was out of rhythm in the talk of Ruby Markowitz's relatives. On instinct, or hunch, Frank Lyons elected to dig further into the death of a man who had distrusted cops all his forty-two years.

Bookmaking is a telephone business, and Markowitz maintained an answering service. As a protection, New York bookies give their clients code names, often in the form of a little joke. To bet $1,000 on the New York Yankees, a client of Markowitz's named, say, Nathan Detroit, might telephone the service and say, "This is Mr. Carr, I want one big unit on the Bombers." In trying to confirm the Williamsburg stories and to understand just how Ruby Markowitz made a living, Detective Lyons found the answering service Ruby had used.

Digging in an upstairs storage room at the service offices, he found a basketful of messages for "Ruby" in October. On the two or three days after Markowitz's death, there had been roughly 150 messages. Dead, Ruby was unable to call clients back or to keep appointments. His clientele had reacted with annoyance, anger, fright and windstorms of phone calls.

One name that appeared frequently before the death—but never after—was Mr. Shore, spelled variously by different message operators as Shore, Shaw and Shor. Through the New York Telephone Company, Lyons traced Mr. Shore-Shaw-Shor to apartment 5B at 406 East Sixty-third Street.

Apartment 5B, a one-bedroom flat, had been rented to a man who called himself William Weissman. Weissman, Detective Lyons learned from the building's rental agent, was a "consulting engineer." Weissman gave as his employer Fein Industries, Inc., on Park Avenue. His credit reference was Mark Fein.

Detective Lyons telephoned Fein Industries, and asked to speak to Weissman.

"Who?" asked the switchboard operator.

"Bill Weissman," Detective Lyons said.

"There's nobody by that name here," the operator said. "Never has been since I've been with the company."

Detective Lyons now had established a connection between Mark Fein, somebody named Bill Weissman and an apartment on Sixty-third Street. But part of his time had to be spent determining that Markowitz had no mob contacts. Another part had to be spent in search of Bill Weissman. For Lyons this was a discouraging period.

Lyons wanted Mark Fein to explain William Weissman, but Fein would not grant him an interview. Lyons could have called on Fein at the Park Avenue cooperative. He could have bullied his way past doormen and attendants, flashing the detective's shield, No. 679. He could have rung the Fein doorbell and, in the presence of dark-haired Nancy Fein, asked questions. But Lyons chose not to, as a matter of personal code. "You don't bust in on the home life of a man with a family unless you're damn sure," he said. When Lyons continued to press for interviews at Fein's office, Fein protested to high officials that the police were harassing him.

Checking all the four hundred messages listed by Markowitz's phone-answering service, Detective Lyons found one left by "Shore" from a Templeton exchange. He traced the number to an apartment ten blocks north on Seventy-third

Street. There Detective Lyons went calling with a partner, gruff general-assignment detective Jimmy Leman. They found Miss Kendal.

The prostitute was not enchanted to greet two detectives at her home and place of business. "No," Gloria, the prostitute, said. "I don't know anybody named Mark Fein."

The detectives pressed a little harder.

"Well," the prostitute said, "actually, there's this friend of mine that does know someone by that name. But she's in Florida now, getting a divorce. She won't be back for a long time."

"What's her name?" Leman said.

"Margaret Foster," Gloria answered. The name came smoothly, because it had been a recent alias.

The detectives left. They were not going to question Gloria Kendal very hard in this first interview. Time was working for them, they believed. There was no point in antagonizing her. They reasoned that Mark Fein, successful businessman, had been having an affair with an apparent prostitute named Margaret Foster. He was also involved in a mysterious apartment. He was not quite the blandly respectable individual that he would have his wife and the police believe. He was a possible, if not a prime, murder suspect. It seemed unlikely that Fein had committed murder himself, but it was possible, faintly possible, that he had hired the gun that did the job.

Every day, as autumn deepened into winter, two men who were becoming deadly adversaries went separate ways to work in New York City. Mark Fein drove down Park Avenue in his white Lincoln Continental. Frank Lyons drove in from a mortgaged house in a Long Island suburb, except when his wife needed the car and he had to take the train.

The stalking was subtle and civilized, not simply because Mark Fein was rich, although that unquestionably had its advantages. Station-house violence has been curtailed in New York since a generation ago, when a murder suspect who cried harassment would have earned himself a beating in the base-ment of some out-of-the-way precinct. ("The whole Fein case might have been solved right there," a retired detective I know remarks wistfully.)

No, there was no chance that Fein would be beaten, and he does not seem to have been afraid of that. Instead, he seems to have looked on Lyons in the same way that he had looked on Markowitz—as someone who had damn well better take off, if he knew what was good for him. Fein might have gotten away with his contempt for Ruby Markowitz had he not compounded it with contempt for Frank Lyons. He did not understand Frank Lyons, who earned less in a year ($9,500) than Fein sometimes bet in a week. It surpassed all Fein's understanding that Detec-tive Lyons could not be laughed at, or swatted away.

The police put Gloria out of work in a calculated, professional manner. Prostitution, like bookmaking, is a telephone business and, since its practitioners go out on house calls or hotel calls, a phone-answering service is important. Detectives persuaded Gloria's service to drop her number from their rolls.

Prostitution is also a referral business. A busy New York City prostitute is sometimes swamped with calls. When that hap-pens, she sends surplus clients to associates. Then, during her own slow weeks, the prostitute benefits from favors returned. Detectives discovered the names of many of Gloria's associates on the East Side of Manhattan. Word spread among them: "Don't send any more customers to Gloria Kendal."

Finally, the detectives began visiting Gloria's apartment, in the sedate and expensive building on Seventy-third, arriving at irregular intervals. Occasionally Gloria was unable to answer the door immediately. The detectives then announced them-selves and knocked loudly. "A decibel rate," one suggests, "just below disturbing the peace."

Devoid of an answering service, deprived of referrals, fre-quently interrupted during working hours, Gloria finally said, in effect, "Goodness gracious." Whereupon she fled the apartment. She was very angry at the police, but not furious. After all, she had not been arrested.

Following Gloria's temporary retirement, Frank Lyons, identifying himself as "Manhattan Homicide," called on the man who owned the building and asked if he could see Gloria Kendal's lease. There was, it developed, no lease in the name of Gloria Kendal. "Not the greatest surprise in history," Lyons said. But there was a lease signed by one Margaret Foster. "Describe Margaret Foster," Detective Lyons asked. Before the landlord had finished, Lyons realized that Margaret Foster and Gloria Kendal were the same person. A little more had come clear. Detective Lyons now had a positive concept of the woman chosen as paramour by Mark Fein of Park Avenue. She was not a Park Avenue lady.

One alias problem solved, police moved on to the others. Who was Mr. Shore-Shaw-Shor? Was he William Weissman? Was there any William Weissman? What was Mark Fein's relationship to this great confusion of names?

Approaching confusion lucidly, Lyons asked a real-estate man to describe William Weissman, as he had asked another real-estate man to describe Margaret Foster. This time matters were not quite so obvious. The second real-estate man had never seen William Weissman. He had only heard about him from Fein. Thinking like a tough, suspicious cop, Lyons decided that William Weissman, whom nobody had ever seen, or spoken to, was probably an alias used by Mark Fein to carry out his affair with the prostitute.

The Shore-Shaw-Shor name, which had first led detectives to the Sixty-third Street apartment of Mark Fein, alias William Weissman, also appeared in answering-service records of the Seventy-third Street apartment of Margaret Foster, alias Gloria Kendal. It began to look as though slight, dapper Mark Fein, all by himself, might be not only William Weissman but also Mr. Shore-Shaw-Shor. Lyons recalls thinking that he would never really be content until he had answered all the questions once and for all. At about this time, Mark Fein, feeling a backlash from the investigation, decided that he would contend with police questions. Fein selected as the scene a Madison Avenue law office. He chose as attorney a former Assistant District Attorney named Albert Blinder. Provided that Blinder remained present throughout, Mark Fein agreed to answer police questions on the morning of December 27, 1963.

Four detectives talked to Fein and the lawyer in the Madison Avenue office that day. At first, Fein tried to be pleasant. He softly reminded the policemen that he was a man who could walk into any bank and get $35,000 on his name alone. Still, he wanted to help the detectives working on the case. He just didn't want to get involved in a scandal because he'd made a few bets.

What about the Sixty-third Street apartment?

Fein knew nothing about it.

The detectives hit Fein with the name "William Weissman." Fein threw his hands into the air and held a private conference with Al Blinder, the lawyer.

What about Margaret Foster?

Who?

The detectives hit Fein with the name of Gloria Kendal. Hands in the air again. Another conference.

He had this friend, Mark Fein explained finally, named Billy Tishman, who ran a furniture store in Harlem. Billy liked to bet, but didn't really have the money. He'd had to help out Billy and a second friend named Robert Katz, after they'd gotten in over their heads with Ruby. They'd liked the Yankees in the last Series.

What about the apartment? the police repeated. What about Gloria Kendal?

"It's Billy's apartment," Mark Fein said, heavily, "and it's Billy's broad."

The friendship between Mark Fein and William Tishman did not survive December 27, 1963. Detective Lyons promptly

sought Tishman and repeated Fein's remark. Tishman red-
dened with fury. He was threatened, he felt. So was his marriage. Damnit, it wasn't his apartment, although he had sold
Fein the furniture for it. Damnit, he didn't know any Gloria.
"Shore," Tishman told Detective Lyons, was the code name
that Ruby, the dead bookie, had given Fein. The bookie's little
joke was that Mark liked the beach. "The joke was Shore, as in
'beach,' get it?" "Yeah," Detective Lyons said, "I get it."

He was closer now, Frank Lyons knew, but a long way from
finished. Other detectives still wanted to classify the Markowitz
murder as a bookie holdup, *cum* homicide. Others liked a gang
theory. And Mark Fein was not encouraging further investigation. He was pressuring the New York City Police Department
to leave him alone.

To Lyons, consumed by his own investigation, the *real* problem was Gloria. She held the key. But once out of the Seventy-
third Street apartment, Gloria had been moving beyond the
district called Manhattan Homicide North. As testimony later
showed, she went to Canada and to the Virgin Islands. As 1964
began, Detective Lyons of Homicide North, had merely a dubi-
ous case and a missing prostitute. He also had an unrelenting
sense that "somehow, in some crazy way, this crazy Fein kid
had something to do with the killing."

The furniture in Mark Fein's bachelor apartment was missing
by the time police found out that the apartment existed. Bill
Tishman, who ran the furniture store in Harlem, had provided
rugs, chairs, sofa and bed to Fein's order, and Tishman was able
to give Detective Lyons a detailed description of every article.
However, he had no idea where "all the stuff has gone."

Two people, Lyons felt, might have put the furniture in storage. One was Fein and the other was Gloria. Accordingly, he
began to look for the furniture under four names: Fein and
Weissman and Kendal and Foster. "Sounds like a mixed law
firm," Lyons says. Armed with the four names and Tishman's

detailed description of the furniture, Detective Lyons began investigating warehouses in Manhattan. After checking about fifteen on a discouragingly long list, he found the furniture. It had been stored, the warehouseman said, after looking at Lyons' gilt shield, by a woman named Kendal.

"Okay," Lyons said. "If you hear from her again, tell her that you can't sell the stuff unless she comes down and gives you her power of attorney. Okay?"

"Yessir, Detective," said the man from the moving company.

Lyons' reasoning, in seeking the furniture, was one more of his cold, professional acts. Gloria was out of business. She might need money. The missing furniture could be a source. It was on February 16, 1964, more than four months after Ruby Markowitz was murdered, that Gloria, back from Canada and the Caribbean, cut off from Mark Fein who had become afraid to see her, cut off from her old trade, phoned the Century Moving & Storage Company in Manhattan. "Please," she said, in her little-girl business tone, "sell my furniture." The man from Century, who wanted no trouble with Homicide, said, "As soon as you come down here and sign a power of attorney." Four days later she did.

Gloria remembered Lyons. He was a cop who hadn't played rough. He'd been one of the guys who drove her from her setup, right off Park Avenue, but he had talked softly and he hadn't arrested her. In her way, considering that he was a cop, Gloria kind of liked Detective Lyons. "How much money do you have on you?" Lyons asked her, when she all but walked into him in front of the Century warehouse. "Oh, hon," Gloria said. "Only about a dollar."

"Well," said Lyons, treating her like a lady, "maybe I better buy you a martini."

Gloria, who had been running too long to suit herself, brightened. "Maybe you better have one," she said. "I'm going to tell you something that'll shock you."

"Guys in my business," said Detective Lyons, "are hard to shock."

"Oh," said Gloria, broke, deserted and challenged. "Mark Fein murdered Ruby. He shot him. I saw the body in a trunk." As he now admits, Detective Frank Lyons *was* shocked. It was the first revelation of the testimony she was to give at the trial.

The arrest came within hours. Detectives Lyons and Leman, knowing Fein's penchant for dining out, drove up Park Avenue at about eight o'clock in the evening. Soon Fein appeared with his wife in the doorway of the apartment building. Fein walked away from Nancy and started toward the garage where he stored his Lincoln. "Mark," Detective Leman said, "you remember me. I'm placing you under arrest for homicide."

Abruptly, Mark Fein, the untouchable, screamed. "Call Al [lawyer Al Blinder]. I'm being kidnaped."

The doormen at 1095 Park heard Mark Fein's cries. Frank Lyons had to move fast to prevent them from obstructing an arrest in a capital crime.

"Look," Lyons yelled, as Nancy screamed and two doormen moved toward him. "Hold it," Lyons shouted. His left hand held his detective's shield. His right hand sat on his gun. "We've made one arrest. We don't want to make any more."

In the car, a few minutes later, Lyons said quietly, "Would you like a cup of coffee, Mark?" The detective felt that maybe, over coffee, Fein might tell the truth.

"Could I have a Scotch?" Fein asked.

"Well, it's going to be a long night," Detective Leman said, "so I guess it'll be okay." Pumping a defendant over coffee is preferable; good lawyers have ways of making conversation over drinks seem suspect. But Leman took what he could get. In the end he found that he'd got nothing, except a tab for two Scotches. Fein drank silently, except when he asked for permission to call his wife. (Leman agreed, and Fein told Nancy to have a lawyer meet him at the precinct house to which he was being taken.)

With Fein imprisoned, his father, Irving, announced to the press that there had been a horrible misunderstanding. Then Irving Fein went out and hired the late William Kleinman to supervise Mark's defense. A deceptively bland man, who wore rimless spectacles and who liked to be called colonel, William Kleinman had the reputation of being one of the ablest criminal lawyers in New York.

The New York County District Attorney's office prepared the case against Fein with particular care, since there was no doubt that Fein would have the best defense that money could buy. At one point Detective Leman grew impatient with Gloria, who, during questioning, showed a penchant for being coy. Leman shouted at her and called her what she was.

"Don't think you can push me around, you Gestapo louse," Gloria said.

"Don't call me a louse," Leman said. Soon Gloria was shouting that she took her whole story back, and before all that was resolved Mark Fein was free on bail.

He was sent back to prison on October 19, 1964, the day he went on trial for murder. It was a long trial. Kleinman spent hours, days, asking Gloria about her background. As he probed, he managed to retain a faint expression of distaste. "How," he was asking the jury, "can you believe a person like this?"

As the trial proceeded, Fein began assuming a characteristic posture. He would lean back in his chair, thrust out his chin and seem, for all the world, to be contemplating the process of justice. Observers had to keep reminding themselves that the smug-looking fellow, leaning back, actually was the defendant.

Nancy Fein offered an alibi for her husband. She testified that Mark had been with her at the time of the shooting. As is his constitutional right, Fein did not take the stand. Later, in a long summation, Kleinman reminded the jury that Thanksgiving was coming. The jury deliberated for two days before filing into the courtroom on November 25.

Fein stood, expectantly, chin still outthrust. "Guilty of murder in the second degree," said the jury foreman. It was a verdict that called for from twenty years to life. The Mark Fein everyone had seen vanished. Smugness drained from him as blood had run out of Ruby Markowitz. While the jurors were polled, Fein slumped. When he was led away, his face was absolutely white.

Professionals feel that Kleinman did a reasonable job in saving his client from a first-degree murder conviction and possible electrocution. "We will appeal," Irving Fein announced and, still going for the best his money could find, hired Louis Nizer to do the job. No matter. Fein went to Sing Sing. Every appeal was defeated. "Now I ask you," Detective Lyons said ironically, "wouldn't it have been cheaper to have paid the bookie?"

It is probably too much to expect the principals in the Fein-Markowitz case to profit from their lessons. They still believe in bookmaking in Williamsburg. There is no indication that Gloria Kendal has joined the Peace Corps. Mark Fein in prison looks sallow, but a psychiatric report says that he appears to be without remorse. It is too much to expect these people to understand that you cannot wander very far from the proven ways of morality without approaching a border of chaos. Although they enacted a modern morality play, they seem not to know it.

But in a small, haunting way, some good did come from this ridiculous murder. On the first anniversary of Markowitz's death, his family invited Detectives Lyons and Leman to a Jewish cemetery, so that they could witness the unveiling of a monument. Lyons' eyes glisten as he talks of Markowitz's twelve-year-old son, praying in Hebrew over the grave. "You know," he says, a little embarrassed, "it was the first time in my life I wore a yarmulke." Well, they asked him to, so maybe they have found something out in Williamsburg.

The Night
They Raided
Academe

They are instantly a nice couple, soft, sensitive, in love and full of hope. She glances at him while she speaks, reassuring herself that he is there. And he waits, pausing after she is silent to be certain that she has finished her thought. Neither means ever to offend.

Their names are important, but best changed here. What happened to them under police assault was frightful and her own actions were somewhat embarrassing. Call them Victor and Celia. These are two young, aesthetic people who are excited at the prospect of a lifetime spent with books. They come from Connecticut, but now they are sitting in the West End Café, a liberal-radical haunt on upper Broadway, and they are at home. He is slim, with gentle, patient eyes and quiet speech. She is more intense, darker, attractive. Her good looks grow on you and take hold.

"A pretty light drink that radicals settle for," I say. We are sitting at a too-small table, across cocktails.

"Oh, it's not so bad," he says.

"I'm not much of a drinker," she says.

Celia works as a secretary in one of the humanities depart-

ments at Columbia. Victor is taking his Ph.D. He has been
working toward the doctorate for six years. Afterward, he will
teach.

"Are you radicals," I ask, "or liberals?"

"We're not very political people," Celia says.

"Well, you're against the war in Southeast Asia."

"Of course," Celia says.

Victor waits. Then he explains. "We're not *active* members
of a formal political group."

"Then how did you get involved with the police?"

Again Victor waits. "Everybody became involved," Celia
says. "You wouldn't have believed what happened. You
couldn't believe it."

"I've seen police in action."

Now Victor volunteers. "Well, then you know."

They are middle-class people who met in college and who
married soon afterward, and she does not mind working as a
secretary now. Later there will be children, and trips to Tangle-
wood and Europe, and one of those gracious large apartments
on Riverside Drive. He will write books, or at least articles, and
she will be hostess. But for the moment they are working their
way upward. They accept the academic system, although they
recognize that it is flawed. Talking to them, you understand
how it was before the bust at Columbia. They are young people,
but already settled, already secure. Security comes early in
academe; it is the narcotic of the professor's trade.

"Some of Victor's friends were young faculty people," Celia
says. "We set up a telephone-relay system. That is, in case the
police were coming, we'd all have certain people to call, to get
them on campus."

"What could you do with cops on campus?" I say.

"The idea," Celia says, "was to have as many faculty bodies
as possible to interpose between the students and the police."

She looks at Victor, who nods. "There was a sense of stability,
too," he says. "The idea was that faculty people and even people

like us, who are not quite faculty but are older than under-
graduates, would be a calming influence."

"And you could bear witness," I say.

Victor and Celia live twenty minutes south of the Columbia
campus, in three rooms of a converted brownstone. They had
been busy all through the week of troubles. On the night of
April 29, 1968, they did a turn of watch on the campus and got
home at about midnight. There were rumors of a bust, but there
had been many rumors before. They went to bed exhausted.
Victor and Celia had been asleep for perhaps an hour when the
telephone rang. It was someone from the relay system. "There
is every indication," the voice said to Victor, "that the police are
about to clear the buildings. Please come to the campus, if
you're willing." Civility in academe. *Please come, but only if.*

The phone had jarred them both awake. Victor put on slacks,
a shirt and a jacket. Celia drew on a pair of black tights, pausing
to straighten the seams. She slipped into a miniskirt and blouse
and pulled a dark kerchief over her head. The evening was
mild. They taxied to the campus, and at the Broadway gate a
professor, whom they recognized, and several policemen,
whom they did not, asked for their identification cards. Inside,
they started toward the flights of steps and the green statue
called Alma Mater standing before Low Library. A man dressed
in a lumberjacket shouted, "Hold it. Hold it. You can't go up
there."

"Are you a policeman?" Celia said.

"Yes, I'm a policeman. And you can't go up there."

The man wore no badge. Celia was not used to being addressed so rudely. She bit her lip.

"Where can we go?" Victor asked.

"Stand over there," the policeman ordered. He pointed
across College Walk toward South Field.

Victor took Celia's arm and gently led her. "Don't let him
bother you," he said.

"He talked as if he owned the place," Celia said.

South Field is bordered by privet, and in the dim light cast from campus lampposts, Victor led Celia through the hedges until they were standing in the open field. On steps above, they could see lines of police moving, silent. Hundreds of other Columbia people had been herded into South Field with them. Victor and Celia stood helpless in the open field, beginning to feel claustrophobic under the cloudy, dark night sky. Then someone came through the hedges shouting, "They've locked the gates. The campus gates are locked. They've sealed the campus."

In the West End bar, among the liberals and the radicals, Celia is telling most of the story, but always looking toward Victor, making sure he is there. It is as if recalling the April night makes terror close, and she needs comfort. I ask if she wants another drink.

"No," says Celia, with soft, black, puppy eyes. "I want to get everything just right, just the way it was."

Low Library was illuminated. They could see that from South Field. A bank of police lights played on the massive Romanesque façade. Although the sight was striking, the lights were there simply to facilitate arrests, and to prevent escape. Sound carried the first hint of violence. Victor and Celia heard sounds rolling from Low Library. Men and women were screaming, in pain, in terror.

"Do something," Celia said.

"We can't," Victor said. "We can't go anywhere. You see those uniformed police." Victor pointed to a line on top of the steps. "They're TPFs, the Tactical Patrol Force. There's no way we can get through."

The screaming rolled down, as if from a madhouse. "You're being used," someone shouted at the TPF patrolmen. "Can't you understand you're being used?" The TPFs faced the crowd in South Field, but you could not make out their faces. It was too dark. All you could see were their bulky forms, their helmets and their nightsticks.

In front of Low, police began dragging students down the

stone steps. One policeman would hold each leg, and then the men backed downstairs rapidly in tandem. At intervals on South Field, you could hear heads slamming rhythmically against the stone. One student was screaming, "I'll walk. I'll walk." Then, as the pain and terror magnified, he lost speech, and made a high shrill horrifying sound.

The crowd on South Field began chanting, "Strike, strike, strike!" A policeman bellowed, "All right, now back up toward that building over there." He indicated Butler Hall. People spun and backed quickly. Celia turned her ankle in the spongy grass. It stung and would hurt more. The crowd was shouting, "Strike, strike!"

No one admits just who gave the order, but suddenly the Tactical Patrol Police charged. "Link arms," someone screamed. "Link arms and they can't move us."

The police held clubs high. The crowd turned and ran. The police beat the retreating people on calves and thighs and buttocks, and poked anyone who turned with the point of a club thrust hard toward the groin.

Celia was running as fast as she could. Her ankle ached. She wanted to tell Victor she had hurt her ankle. They were running toward the southwest corner of the campus. They had been standing where the police told them to stand. They had not been asked to leave. They had not been warned. And now they were running toward an exit at a corner of the campus. But the campus was locked tight. Celia stopped for an instant. She still heard the shrieking from Low. It was just wrong.

"Motherfuckers," she screamed at the TPFs. "Motherfucker fascist pigs."

"You know," Victor says in the West End Café, "I've never seen her like that. Never. Ever."

Policemen chased her. She was terrified now. They would beat her, Celia thought. The soft, puppy eyes were wild. The injured ankle made her limp. Running awkwardly, Celia fell over a small fence that protected flowers. Her tights snared.

Celia felt she could not move. A policeman began bending her legs backward, against the hip joint, as if to force her heels against the back of her neck. He had a square hard face; his lips were drawn across set teeth.

"Let go of me," Celia screamed. "Let go, you motherfucker." The policeman's eyes were small and very bright.

Victor was trying to help her, but a plainclothesman beat a nightstick at Victor's back. Victor turned. "I'm trying to help my wife."

The word was shocking. This woman, draped brazenly across the fence, was a wife. The policeman took his hands off her legs. Then he and Victor helped her up. Celia was crying with fright.

Five feet from where she stood, students crouched in a circle shouting, "It's our university, it's our university."

"Bastard kids," roared the policeman. He whipped out hand- cuffs and charged. He held one cuff and swung the other. A boy yelped and collapsed holding his nose.

It was still dark. Celia was screaming and shrieking. Victor fixed on an objective, a building beyond the battle.

He led her firmly and they made good progress, but a few yards away from the entrance, Victor saw a boy who had been brutalized. Blood ran from a scalp cut. So much blood ran down his eyes that he could not see. The boy was very young, proba- bly a freshman. He was wailing over and over, "Somebody help me."

A uniformed policeman watched clinically. "You have to get him to a doctor," Victor said.

"*You* get him to a doctor," the cop said.

Victor took the dark kerchief that was still on Celia's head. She was crying less loudly now. He wiped the boy's bloody eyes and pressed the kerchief against the wound. Then, taking his weeping wife with one arm and the weeping freshman with the other, Victor led them to a door into New Hall, a men's resi- dence.

They had not gone very far through the glass doors, the

graduate student, the bloody freshman and the weeping wife, when a Columbia security man ran toward them from within. Victor offered a small smile of welcome.

"Hey," the guard said. "You can't come in here."

"Why not?"

"No women in the men's dormitories after ten o'clock."

They are holding hands at the table. The remembered experience has brought them very close together. "It was ten days before I could go back to the campus," Celia says, "but I'm pretty well over this now."

"I got her to bed and asleep and I went back," Victor says. "I saw an overrun first-aid station. Did you know about that?"

"I know the doctor who was overrun."

"That morning," Victor says, "Lionel Trilling was standing on the steps, looking at all the wreckage. A wonderful critic, a person like that. He seemed in shock. He was stooped and gray and crushed, as though *he* had been beaten."

The policeman is sitting in a bar on Broadway, fourteen blocks from the Columbia campus, remembering some of the things he saw and did. "Go slow, very slow," the cop says. "Don't try and push me." Then: "Hell, I shouldn't even be talkin' to you at all."

The police, the best of them, are not proud of what they did during the Battle for Morningside Heights. Jacques Nevard, a former deputy commissioner for public relations, submits, "We were asked to step into the worst kind of scene—a dispute among Columbia and its students and its neighbors. Any cop will tell you there's nothing worse than breaking up a family quarrel." A Captain Glaser in Nevard's office adds, "I wouldn't repeat to you some of the things they called our men." But in the end one leaves police headquarters certain that important cops are unhappy. They feel that there is nothing much to choose between radicals and academicians. They are only sorry they had to make the choice.

The policeman at the bar is an off-duty plainclothesman, identifiable as police by an assertive manner and by a bulge on his right hip. "You want a Scotch?" I ask.

"No. I drink beer."

The policeman is a stocky, black-haired Irishman, a bachelor of thirty-two, and he is worried lest I print his name.

"You can say I'm Irish," he says. "They ain't gonna identify me from that, but if you say who I am, you know, it starts some heat."

"Sure."

"It's better for you if you don't use my name. If you promise you won't use it, I can tell you more about what really went on."

"Well, sure. I promise."

The beer comes. The cop sips. He smacks his lips and sips again. "Good," he says. "What did they tell you downtown?"

"Not a helluva lot."

"They don't know what's going on downtown."

It is a reasonable gripe of a workingman against his superiors. And this cop is a workingman. He works hard for a base of $8,700. He supplements it, I suppose, in little ways, as policemen do, but he is not wealthy. "Did you go to college?" he asks me.

"Until I started writing."

"I got in a term at St. John's. Then I had to quit and join the force. My father was dead. Believe me, I wished I coulda finished. If I had college, I coulda gone to law school. That woulda been something for my mother. It would have made her proud to have me be an Assistant DA." The cop is sipping as he talks. He chain-smokes cigarettes without a filter. "What I saw at the college was something terrible," he says.

"What college?"

"Columbia College. Kids acting like bums, and showing no respect for the law. These same kids who shoulda been down on their knees thanking the Lord that He had let them go to college. I woulda been on my knees myself."

More beers come. The cop grows expansive. "I get kinda sore at something, you know? Everything I got in life I worked for. It gets me sore when I see these kids, who been handed every-thing, pissing it away, talking like bums, dressing like pigs."

"Did they *call* you pig?"

He has black eyes; they glare like lamplights. "Where'd you hear that? It's some joke, ain't it, a rich kid calling a police officer pig. These smart-ass college kids think they're so big they can get away with anything they want. I don't have to take that, particularly from smart-ass college kids."

His jaw is set. He rages with remembered anger. "But you agree to take certain abuse," I say, "when you sign up to be a cop."

"All right," he says. "But I got limits. My mother doesn't have to take abuse." He continues very quietly and evenly.

"I'm up at Columbia. I'm trying to get people moving. They're maybe not moving. I'm a little scared myself. Not much, but a little. And I gotta shove. I shove. There's some girl sitting down. I tell her, *'Move.'* She sits where she is and she looks at me and says—wait a minute. I wrote it down." The cop reaches into his wallet and takes out a folded piece of white paper.

"I wrote it down, in case I ever got to testify on any of the stuff that went on." He stares at the worn paper and reads: "Your sister sucks off your mother." He reads it in a monotone. Then he carefully replaces the paper in the wallet.

"So I hit her," he says. "I hit her good. I made her cry."

Avery Hall, housing the architecture students, was the first building that the police had to attack frontally in the small hours of April 30. The main police column approached along College Walk, then turned north past Low Plaza. Scores and then hun-dreds of observers trailed the police.

Avery stands thirty yards northeast of Low. At 3 A.M. the grounds before Avery lay in darkness. The brightest light issued from illuminated fountains, dry now, at Uris Hall. The police took darkness as their shield.

Hedges border a plaza before the doors to Avery. Silently, plainclothesmen moved in, columns of bulky men tramping along the hedge rows. About one hundred uniformed police massed before the doors. Behind, wedging them, a crowd grew to about nine hundred.

The young people jeered and chanted. "Cops must go. Cops go home." In front of the police, men stood in a silent cordon. Alongside students, professors of architecture were there: Percival Goodman, Alexander Kouzmanoff, Raymond Lifchez. From the second floor of Avery rock music blared. The police felt uncomfortable, alien, somewhat frightened. A university spokesman and a police officer read a demand that those occupying Avery Hall leave it. While the policeman was talking, someone in the cordon broke and cut into the hedges. Plainclothesmen beat him with saps. A sap is a small truncheon sheathed in leather. It does not break the skin the way a blackjack does, but it inflicts equal pain.

The men in the cordon locked arms and sang "We Shall Overcome." "Get 'em, get the Commies," someone shouted. The men continued to sing:

> Deep in our hearts
> Thy will be done,
> We shall overcome . . .

A police charge stifled the hymn. The uniformed police advanced, throwing people aside toward the hedges where the plainclothesmen waited with saps. One man was lifted and thrown completely over a hedge. A woman, standing in front of the building, was spun, her arms twisted behind her back. She screamed and screamed. Some uniformed police lashed out with walkie-talkie aerials. The advancing police did not trample this cordon so much as punish it. A professor staggered out of the mass, bleeding from the head. He fell across a concrete pavement, moaning. Professor Lifchez was beaten until he could not stand or walk. The police were unidentifiable in the darkness. They had no one to account to. And they were scared. The elements mixed to a ferocity.

Police burst into the foyer of Avery. A small group sat there. The police grabbed the students and shoved them into the darkness outside where others were still beating professors.

A police vanguard drove up five flights. The sixth floor was dark and empty. The police cast their flashlights down corridors and went to the fifth floor. There they found a group singing. Others ran down farther. Near the second floor, on the marble staircase, Robert Thomas, Jr., a district reporter for the *New York Times*, was watching.

Police were pouring into Avery. "Hey, what are ya doing?" someone shouted at Thomas.

"I'm with the *Times*."

"No press," a policeman shouted. "No goddamn press."

Police began to swing at Thomas. The reporter found his press card, a little colored cardboard badge signed by Howard Leary, the Police Commissioner, and, spinning and tumbling down the stairs, he held it as high as he could. It was no armor. A policeman swung a handcuff into Thomas' scalp. Twelve stitches later closed the wound.

A gantlet formed. The police on the fourth and fifth floors handcuffed students to one another and started them down the stairs. Farther down, other police kicked them. Some stumbled. The police kept prodding.

One protester, semiconscious and bleeding from the head, was dragged down the outside steps of Avery, feet first, by a policeman.

"Can't you see?" a young woman screamed. "That's a human being you're doing that to."

The policeman never looked up. "He could walk if he wanted to," he said.

Another girl, in jeans, kicked out as a policeman dragged her outside. Two plainclothesmen pulled her to a tree in the court-yard and they rhythmically beat her head against the trunk. "Fuck you," she yelled. "Oh, fuck you, you bastards. Oh."

Two men moved to her rescue. Plainclothesmen grabbed them and pulled them down. One of the men screamed as saps landed. The sound of saps continued. Avery was cleared in twenty minutes. By 3:20 A.M. the Architecture commune had been destroyed.

Mathematics was the last to fall. Across campus from Avery, this commune, mixing a hard-line radical student core with a good number of visiting adults, had devised a rigorous defense. Each step on the staircase was slicked with soap or vaseline. Activists on the second and third floors stood ready with chairs. As the police scrambled up, those who did not slip would be bombarded.

A contingent of 150 policemen reached Math at 3:45 A.M. A conservative claque followed the police, calling, "Go get 'em." Conservatives climbed the steps of Earl Hall, southeast of Math, for a better view of police massing. Between the buildings, Brooke G. Schoepf, a medical anthropologist, and Robert Furtz, a fourth-year student at Columbia Medical School, spread white blankets on the lawn. A young physician named Desmond Callan and a medical orderly named Kelly Snodgrass joined them. A police officer approached and said, not harshly, "You better not stand here. You'll get run over." The four moved the aid station to what they hoped would be a safe position. Even before the police moved, they had a patient. One boy, standing in the faculty-student cordon outside the building, watched the police assemble and began to cry. He was treated for "an acute anxiety reaction"—hysterics.

Fifty plainclothesmen milled near the aid station. They wore no badges. Instead, they had buttons of green. The buttons told other police that they were colleagues but protected anonymity. "Hey," a plainclothesman shouted to Miss Schoepf, who was wearing a white jacket. "They're gonna need you soon."

A reporter from the FM radio station WBAI arrived, bleeding from a scalp wound. Callan examined him and cleaned the injury. The reporter, carrying a portable tape recorder, continued to describe the scene.

"You'd better lie down on a blanket and take it easy," Callan said, "until the bleeding stops."

A police officer, seeing the tape recorder, told the reporter, "Okay. Move."

"This man is injured," Dr. Callan said. "He should not be moved."

"If this man stays," said the policeman, "I'll clear the whole lot of you out of here."

The reporter staggered away.

Spotlights played on the area. You could see the action at Math clearly. A group of newspaper reporters stood behind the police. From the steps of Earl Hall, the conservatives shouted, "Get 'em." The administration warrant to clear the building was read through bullhorns. From the fourth floor of Math someone leaned out and shouted, "Fuck you, cops." A group called in unison, "Up against the wall, motherfuckers." The police did not respond.

The front door was barricaded and chained shut. Policemen pried the door with crowbars and used a small saw to cut the chains. When the doors opened, the police confronted a towering stack of furniture. The Math radicals foraging in many offices had created the greatest of all barricades. Still the police worked quickly. The forward men disentangled pieces of the barricade, mostly chairs, and passed them back. Other police set them on the sidewalk. If you could forget what you had seen at Avery, you might have thought you were observing a model police action.

But the police were still nervous about being wedged. A ranking officer approached a line of TPFs and pointed toward the conservative students standing on the steps of Earl Hall. "All right," he said. "Clear 'em out."

The TPFs bolted up the steps of Earl toward the young men who had been urging the police, "Go get 'em."

You could hear individual shouts. "No, no. Not us. We're with you."

"Hey, what are you doing? We're on your side."

The charging TPFs closed with the conservatives. One neatly dressed boy was thrown against a hedge, his crew-neck sweater torn. He lay trembling. Other TPFs approached. "I'm with *you,*" the boy screamed. Then he lunged to his feet and ran.

Inside Math, the police made their way up the soapy stairs very slowly, some on all fours. From above, students threw chairs. The police backed away.

An officer shouted through a bullhorn, "Anyone throwing chairs will be charged with assaulting an officer. *Assaulting an officer.* You can go to jail for ten years." The barrage stopped. The police resumed their climb. On the second floor, students, among them the chair throwers, waited. From higher still, you could hear *"Up against the wall . . ."*

The police seized the protesters, some of whom fought back, and shoved them down the slippery stairs. Radicals skidded and bounced to the ground floor. There they were handcuffed and hurled outside. The police there had heard about the chair throwing. They used blackjacks and clubs against the handcuffed students. Sometimes as many as four pummeled one. "You're not supposed to beat them," one girl shouted. "You're not supposed to do that." A uniformed policeman turned and yelled at her: "We'll show these black-white motherfuckers to tangle with us."

The beatings continued. They were not worse than the beatings elsewhere, only more visible. By 4 A.M. Math was cleared. The police had done the job they were hired to perform. But they were not finished. Police rage was far from spent.

Dr. June Finer had set up her aid station on South Field.

Victor and Celia were standing there. So were conservative students, frightened now. The reigning mood of the South Field crowd was to protest. No one knows how many people filled the field; estimates run from fifteen hundred to two thousand, and walking among them you could hear shouts of outrage.

"Hey, what are you doing on my campus?"

"Cops must go."

"Cops eat shit."

"Up against the wall."

After a while one chant became most common. The Columbia crowd bellowed at the police: *"Sieg heil! Sieg heil! Sieg heil!"*

A few minutes after four, the police began their charge. They overran June Finer's aid station and they knocked over a man in a white jacket who shouted, "No. I'm a doctor."

The police advanced, whipping the nightsticks their inspectors promised Columbia executives would be left in the station houses. They picked individuals at random, boys and girls, men and women, and beat them. You heard the sounds and after a time you could distinguish between nightstick and blackjack against flesh. The crowd shrank toward the library, 375,000 volumes strong, named for Nicholas Murray Butler. The building was locked. The books inside were safe.

The police, arrayed in a loose picket line, drove the crowd toward a gate on West 114th Street, bolted earlier to prevent the escape of protesters. Panicked people managed somehow to climb these gates, which are ten feet tall. Then, for no apparent reason, they rushed toward Broadway. One policeman, standing on the corner of Broadway and 114th, started as he saw a crowd of ragged, panicked Columbia people hurrying toward him. "Hey," he shouted in alarm, "just what the hell is going on in there?" No one could tell him because no one had yet realized that at Columbia the police had now become the rioters.

IV
The Flower
of the Field

All flesh is grass, and all the goodliness
thereof is as the flower of the field.
                                        ISAIAH

The World
of John Lardner

On a Vermont hillside, five months after John Lardner died at the age of forty-seven, Robert Frost mentioned Lardner's name and made a request. "When you get back to New York," Frost said, "tell this fellow Lardner that I think he has a very unusual slant on things. Comical. Tell him I like his stuff. But be careful now. Don't embarrass him with praise."

Frost was eighty-five then and still too youthful, too concerned with the issues of life, to devote much time to reading obituaries. I could not bring myself to tell the poet that Lardner was dead. Instead, on that high hill, I thought how much this compliment, from one believer in understatement to another, would have meant to John. It certainly pleased his friends. One, who had been a sportswriter, heard of it and said intensely, "That's the way it should be. Cabbies and fighters liked my stuff. Robert Frost liked his."

Although most perceptive sportswriters accepted him as matchless, the craft of John Lardner cannot properly be said to have been sportswriting. Nor was it profile writing, nor column writing. After the painstaking business of reportage, his craft was purely writing: writing the English sentence, fusing sound and meaning, matching the precision of the word with the rhythm of the phrase. It is a pursuit which is unfailingly demanding, and Lardner met it with unfailing mastery. This is not to bracket him with Sean O'Casey and T. S. Eliot, who also wrote English sentences in his time, 1912 to 1960. John chose his arena, created his world within carefully reasoned limits. I think it is fair to say that within these limits, in his time, he had no equal.

The world of John Lardner was a place of grace and humor, where no one was as evil as Iago or as virtuous as St. Joan, and where it always seemed that everyone talked softly. Unobtrusively, in a corner near the bar, house rules were posted in a few lines of small type. They went along these lines: "Living is difficult at times and three out of three people die, but there is not much sense in railing against either. Deal, drink, or read, but do it quietly." It was a pleasant place, without hot tears or strident laughter.

Heroes in his world were gamblers who fleeced innocents, ball players whose ignorance sang, and prizefighters who attempted to father a large portion of their country. The villains, at first thought, seemed very much the same, but there was a fine and unwavering difference. Lardner once explained why he liked an avaricious baseball promoter named Branch Rickey and disliked an avaricious baseball promoter named Walter O'Malley. "They do the same things," Lardner said, "but O'Malley won't admit it."

Because the world seen through Lardner's writing was such an enjoyable place, great numbers of people pressed to meet its creator. I don't know what they expected. Possibly Lardner entering with a soft-shoe routine, while Battling Siki, the Senegalese light heavyweight, sparred in one wing and Titanic Thompson, the infinite hustler, booked bets in the other.

What they found was a tall, bespectacled man, black-haired and not very comfortable with strangers. Lardner spoke sparely to people he did not know, and it was amusing to watch editors and others cope with silence on first meeting Lardner. Commonly they threw a few of their favorite anecdotes, then slipped into banalities. I can think of several austere types, unused to silence, remarking to Lardner that Mickey Mantle was a good hitter, or that battle tested a man's courage, or that yessir, it certainly had been hot and here it was only June. As I say, it amused me and I imagine it amused John, too, because he listened carefully, solemnly and kindly. The silence itself was a kindness. John's wit, turned on a cliché, struck sparks.

It was a foolish but understandable error to think one could gain entry into Lardner's world by meeting the man. The world did not exist in the places and things John liked: not in the Artist and Writers Restaurant, where John enjoyed himself standing at the bar sipping Scotch and soda, nor in Saratoga, where he enjoyed himself on those days when his horses won, nor in St. Petersburg, where he enjoyed himself when the springtime sun burned bright. The world existed within Lardner's mind.

This is a point which many people who do not write find puzzling. I suppose some burst into the Mermaid Tavern looking for Hamlet or Antony and, finding only a bald, bearded playwright, left disappointed. I suppose some asked Herman Melville, "Where do you keep the whale?" A puzzling point, perhaps, but a critical one. For the writer lives in no special physical world. Before him lies only what lies before everyone else. The writer's art begins with his own interpretation and imagination. It is to take the world that has been thrust upon him and from it to create a world beyond, more enticing and more real.

How? Lardner could not have told you, nor could Freud. One knows only that this creation is a private act of the mind. At its highest, it cannot be achieved in editorial meetings or in story conferences. It is achieved by one man working alone.

For reasons that he did not bother to make explicit, Lardner never worked for any of Henry Luce's magazines. In the course of earning a living, he worked for several magazines which he did not respect or did not take seriously, but always with the proviso that they not be published by Luce. I think this was an intensely individualistic protest by an intensely individualistic man.

After sparring with Harvard and living in France briefly, he became a reporter on the New York *Herald Tribune.* While still in his mid-twenties, he left the paper to write a syndicated sports column, and presently *Newsweek* hired him to write a sports column once a week. Then came his World War II correspondence. After that there was scarcely a magazine in the country that did not want Lardner's stories on Lardner's terms. (The reference is to style here, not cash.)

It was a memorable career, and at the end Lardner occasionally had to beat off editors with bottles of club soda lest he find himself writing stories he didn't like, or didn't have time for, or couldn't afford. Yet, while Lardner grew successful by writing in his own original, individual way, magazines, generally, became less interested in original, individual articles. *Time* and the *Reader's Digest,* edited up or down to a single level, edited to read as though they had been written by one man, came to be journalistic giants. At least they made gigantic sums of money.

Like any careful writer, Lardner took editing badly, and when someone casually changed a word he had struggled to find, or a viewpoint he had formed slowly, John burned with a quiet, enduring rage. Once an editor ordered him to write that Lew Hoad, the Australian tennis player, was as good as Pancho Gonzales, the American. "Grmmmf," Lardner said but made no further comment until eight months later when Gonzales had beaten Hoad decisively in a hundred-match series. He then spoke of the editor more extensively. "I told the son of a bitch he was wrong eight months ago," Lardner said.

Lardner the journalist moved against the tide of the times and, through something approaching genius, triumphed over the tide. By not working for Luce, who had produced the fad for group journalism, he was registering a protest vote on behalf of others who had been swept along. With the advent of *Sports Illustrated*, which might have allowed him some stylistic range, the protest became costly. Lardner stuck to it as a matter of integrity; he guarded his integrity in a fierce, uncompromising way.

He also stuck to journalism, which troubled certain friends. "You ought to write a novel," people told him from time to time, and Lardner's answer, when he bothered to make one, was a defense of the essay. One evening three of us argued about the form of writing that is most natural. Two held out for poetry, and having Lardner two to one, we moved in with broad, positive statements. Full-arm blows, fight writers call this sort of attack.

"Let's consider primitives," someone said. "Children are primitives, and what do they respond to? Rhyme and meter."

"All right, consider primitives," Lardner said. "The Rosetta Stone was an essay."

John was an essayist in an era of novel worship, an individual journalist in a time of group journalism. That's two strikes, but until the night he died, no one ever slipped a third strike past Lardner. In any time, under any rules, his craft would have carried him to a unique and solitary place, just as it did in the difficult times in which he happened to live.

I knew him for the last five years of his life, when, I suppose, he was dying. He had fought off tuberculosis, but multiple sclerosis was attacking his coordination and episodes of angina stabbed his heart. In addition, his marriage had soured. Still, one never thought of him as sick, or even troubled.

He appeared at *Newsweek* near 4 P.M. each Thursday, with a two-and-a-half-page essay in hand. Then we rode off to the Artist and Writers Restaurant, where he drank steadily, without visible effect, except that after four or five he leaned a bit. I was young and did not understand why finishing the *Newsweek* piece did not leave him ebullient. It did not occur to me that he had already begun wondering about the next one.

We played an intricate game those Thursday twilights. One

of us would quote lines from James Shirley, or from an obscure work by a more famous poet. The other was to continue the poem. Once after *I'd* had four or five, I blurted, *"When I behold, upon the night's starred face."* Lardner refused to respond. Keats' sonnet on death was too obvious. "I move for a disqualification," he said.

We talked mostly about sports and writing. His mind, his world, never ceased to grow and toward the end he mentioned an idea that was developing. "A fiction thing."

"You yielding to the novel?"

"Sort of. Set in the 1920s. Use Dempsey's career as backdrop. Did you know my father lost $500 betting on Willard?"

But already sickness was foreclosing his time. When Dr. Louis Siltzbach told him to quit smoking, Lardner switched to a pipe. "I don't puff it," he said. "It's a prop." Later a heart seizure sent him briefly to Mount Sinai Hospital, where I brought a fifth of Scotch one Sunday. He was offended. Sick or well, he disliked handouts. He indicated the night table. "I've got plenty of my own in there."

"Well, drink it when you get home then," I said.

"I have plenty at the house, too."

"But, John, the thing is gift wrapped."

He nodded slightly. "I guess I can use it in transit. Drink it in the taxi going home."

A few days after his discharge, he began an essay on F.P.A., Franklin Pierce Adams, who had died after several sad years in a West Side nursing home. Lardner was trying his fourth version of an opening paragraph when violent chest pains interceded. By the time Lou Siltzbach reached the apartment on West Twelfth Street, Lardner lay beyond medical help. Toward midnight, he seemed to die.

Siltzbach applied heart massage. Lardner's eyes flickered. "John," the doctor cried, through tears, "you can't die. You're a noble man."

Lardner looked up. "Oh, Lou," he said. "That sounds like a quotation." Then death came.

Now of John Lardner, the writer, I think of a few lines, not from an essay, but from a poem:

> The lyf so short,
> The craft so long to lerne . . .

I am not going to tell you where that's from. John would have known, and this chapter is for him.

The Robinsons

I

This poem
is
a death chant
and a gravestone and a prayer for young Jackie Robinson
who walked among us with a wide stride
moving   moving   moving
through blood and mud and shit of Vietnam
moving   moving   moving
through blood and mud and dope of America

Ethridge Knight, who himself is recovering from heroin addiction, had written these words through tears and reworked the lines many times and, now that he had copied them in careful longhand on yellow paper, he bowed his large dark head and showed them deferentially. Ethridge is groping back toward manhood at Daytop in Seymour, Connecticut, the institution where young Jackie Robinson made himself whole in the brave late years of a brief life.

"It's fine, Ethridge," I said. A faint pained smile. "It moves me." Ethridge Knight, a published poet, is a resident of Daytop. He has stopped taking drugs, but he has not yet reached "confirmation," the day when he is pronounced competent to re-enter the world beyond. His judges, the people who run Daytop, are all former skin-poppers and mainliners. Junkies.

"Thanks, Ethridge," said Jimmy DeJohn, black-goateed and squat as a linebacker. He is an assistant director of Daytop and twenty-four years old. "You can go back to work." Ethridge drifted off soundlessly. "We don't talk about Jackie too much with the residents," DeJohn said. "It upsets them. They can't bear it."

The summer of 1971 was sitting on the Housatonic River and on the valley cottages where one could find the pallbearers for Jackie Robinson, Jr.: careworn George Tocci; Eddie Brown, eight years a Marine; and DeJohn, who was married in a Catholic church in the autumn of 1970, with young Jack as best man. "A few people were surprised to see a black guy best man at an Italian wedding," he said, "but the maid of honor, who was white, was proud to walk down the aisle of St. Margaret Mary's with someone that fine. And I was damn proud." Jimmy shook his head.

The summer day and death talk made incongruity. Nearby corn had grown man-high and in the river, beyond the curving blacktop, someone had anchored a jump and you could hear the skiers on the water, their voices exultant in youth. Summer and death and youth and death; equations reason cannot solve.

The death facts may be stated simply. On June 17, 1971, at about 2:30 A.M., Jackie Robinson, Jr. was found dead in the remnant of a yellow MG. He had driven off the Merritt Parkway at such high speed that the car, which belonged to his brother David, demolished four heavy guard posts. The engine came to rest a hundred feet from the chassis, which looked like a toy car bent double by the hammer of a petulant child. Only wire wheels remained intact. Police theorized that death was instantaneous. Both legs were severed at the knee. The coroner fixed cause as a broken neck. David Robinson identified the car and his brother's body. Jackie Robinson, Sr., fifty-two, broke the news to his wife, assistant professor of psychiatric nursing at Yale.

Newspapers filled their obituaries with fragments of a molten life:

> The late Mr. Robinson, wounded in action in Vietnam, was the son of the first Negro to play in the major leagues. After his discharge the younger Robinson was twice arrested on charges growing from heroin addiction. Later he was said to have ceased using drugs. At the time of his death, he was employed as assistant regional director of Daytop, Inc. Police found neither drugs nor evidence of continuing drug use on the corpse.

"We both came in here September 1968," said Jimmy De-John, "which made us close. And we were dope fiends and we licked it together. He was interested in philosophy. He liked Gibran. And music. Herbie Mann. His bag was helping street people and he was getting to be *some* speaker. That's what he did. Spoke. His dream was having his own community center in a bad ghetto."

The Daytop centers—there are only two in Connecticut—attack addiction through self-confrontation. The approach echoes Jung, who wrote of destruction and rebirth, and even shadows Socrates in the agora, speaking his willingness to die many times. Withdrawal from heroin, say Daytop people, is *not* physical torture. It produces sweating, restlessness and the symptoms of intestinal flu for seventy-two hours. But the idea of convulsing spasms and shrieking agony is decried as the stuff of bad Sinatra pictures and of people who lean on bad Sinatra pictures to cop out. (Withdrawal from *barbiturate* addiction—heroin is a *narcotic*—is described as another problem, truly hideous.)

The addict entering Daytop quits cold. His system recovers quickly, but it takes a year or even two to make an emotional adjustment. A Daytop resident lives in a dormitory with others, and plants corn, works lathes, writes poems. Part of the days are given to talk, in which one is encouraged, figuratively whipped, to face himself. Images shatter. People cry. Although the cure ratio is 80 percent, it is not a gentle place. Young Jackie Robinson ran no gentle road to find Daytop.

He was born in 1946, after the thrilling season when his father broke through baseball's cotton curtain on the way to becoming a Brooklyn Dodger. In succeeding years little Jack became a darling of the Dodger entourage. I have before me a *Life* photograph taken by Nina Leen which shows Jackie sitting on a tricycle before a Brooklyn stoopfront. His father looks on with intent pride; Rachel, his mother, smiles contained, as is her way. The little boy is wearing a white playsuit. Perched surely, no hands, he drinks a glass of milk. It is a pretty picture suggesting contentment, but at the time it was taken people still chuckled as they remembered a remark by Al Smith, the politician: "The only trouble with kittens and pickaninnies is that they grow up."

As young Jackie Robinson moved past three-wheelers, black resistance formed. The point, an arrow of dark fire, was Jackie's father. The big man beat off mixed hatred and scorn: bean balls, obscenities, a too-small salary, a righteous, condescending press. But after he had broken through, Alan Paton made a pilgrimage to shake big Jack's gnarled hand. Earl Warren sprawled in a private box at Ebbets Field, sipping a drink and cheering "my fellow Californian." Two years after that Earl Warren's court struck against school segregation.

When I was traveling with the Dodgers in 1953, Jackie Robinson remarked that he missed being home and the chance to watch his children change day by day. In 1955 he built an estate in a corner of North Stamford, Connecticut, where blacks had come only as servants. This must have made a paradoxical boyhood for young Jackie, pampered by strangers, attacked by bigotry once removed, with an adoring father who went away every other day (it seemed) to play in St. Louis, Cincinnati or Pittsburgh. Still, when the father retired from baseball in 1956, young Jackie cried.

With adolescence, disaffection entered. Young Jack performed poorly in junior high school and went off to prep. He dropped out and enlisted in the Army. He wanted to achieve discipline, he said.

In Vietnam he became a good rifleman. Once as his platoon sat panting on a hummock near Pleiku, he heard a sound and turned and fired a burst from his M–14. Two Vietcong fell dead. A third crawled into undergrowth. The men of the platoon rushed up and slammed his back and yelled, "Nice shooting, Jackie." He nodded and walked slowly to the corpses. He was surprised that they were younger than himself.

Later the platoon was pinned and as mortar fragments fell some men began to cry. Fragments killed the soldier next to Jackie, who himself took shrapnel in the hip. Afterward he put down the incident as "the time I got shot in the ass." But it was in Vietnam that he turned to heroin.

"When he came to Daytop, he was very inward," Jimmy DeJohn said, "and he had hang-ups. He knocked his family as middle-class. I'm middle-class myself. I grew up next to a golf club outside Hartford. I started drinking cough syrup with codeine and getting stuff out of Darvon pills when my father died, but that's another story and you came to talk about Jackie."

DeJohn, Tocci, Brown and I were sitting in a bare office at Daytop. Above DeJohn a sign hung, white paint on brown wood: "J. ROBINSON."

"That's from when he was night mayor," Tocci said. "The staff man in charge late is the night mayor. He seemed to like that when he had kicked it and started working here. That was the sign we hung when he was night mayor."

"A good ball player," DeJohn said. "Batted lefty. He hit a softball a helluva way. But he didn't care for it. After him and me was making progress and going places, people who met him said, 'You're the ball player's son.' He'd say, 'Baseball's not my thing.' Then he'd say, 'Don't use the whole name. Just introduce me as Jackie.' "

"The street people got to be his thing," Tocci said. "He'd go to Hartford, Waterbury, New Haven, where there were bad slums, and tell them about staying away from heroin, and about Daytop."

"No shirt and tie like at home," DeJohn said. "He wore dashikis. Still, he always had good communication with his mother."

"Did he talk to you about his time in Vietnam?"

"I was there," Eddie Brown said. "Long time back—'65. They had us fighting with World War II gear. Jackie talked about the country more than the war." Eddie Brown is short and wide, with wrestler's muscles and a curling scar on his right cheek. "First thing kind of flipped him was it was a different world. Like a woman wants to pee. It don't matter if she's fifteen or seventy, or at the crossroads of town. Up comes the skirt and she lets go."

"About fighting," I said.

"You got to go on these missions, search and destroy, you get high. Booze, hash, whatever. Grass got me a dishonorable discharge. Now when Jackie told me about shooting this burst and finding out he'd killed kids, I asked him what he thought. He said he thought nothing. He made his mind go blank."

"So maybe it was deeper," George Tocci said, "stirring him up when he got back. You're a writer. Couldn't that be possible?"

"It could be possible, sure."

"Mr. Robinson was very nice to us," DeJohn said. "He had us over to his estate and football's my bag and he reached into his trophy case and took out a white football a lot of people had signed. This musta been some kind of an award."

"Before baseball he was a great running back," I said.

"I told him we couldn't use that one, but Mr. Robinson

wanted us to go ahead. And before we were through kicking it around, every signature was rubbed off. Mr. Robinson laughed and said he was just happy to see young people playing ball around his house."

"Did Jackie come to appreciate what his father had done in baseball?"

"Not really," DeJohn said, "but he was coming to appreciate him as a man."

"He found out his dad didn't always have the good life," Tocci said, "that when Mr. Robinson was young his people were so poor dinner would sometimes be a sugar sandwich."

"That started things opening," DeJohn said. "It got better and better between him and his Dad and last year Mr. Robinson had a party for Daytop and he and Jackie hugged each other."

"Wonderful people," Tocci said.

"Jackie won this great victory over heroin," DeJohn said, "and we used to talk—like I say, we're both twenty-four—about the greater victories ahead."

It struck me then to stand up and ask to meet young Jackie Robinson. But of course I could not. He was dead.

On his funeral day, June 21, the coffin lay open. The family had abandoned the suburbs for the services and chosen Antioch Baptist Church on Greene Avenue in Brooklyn. In the 1930s, my great-grandmother owned a house on Greene Avenue where I was taken, very young, to squirm in dark-wood rockers and hear, "You dasn't do that, sonny. Gawd will punish you." Now along Greene the houses decay and all the people are black, except at token public buildings being constructed by whites from segregated unions.

"*In Memoriam,*" said the program, "*Jack Roosevelt Robinson, Jr., 1946–1971.*" I looked up. An open coffin downs hard. When we heard my wife gasp, Al Silverman, then the editor of *Sport,* and I made heavy funeral gossip. There was Hugh Morrow from Nelson Rockefeller's office. Would the Governor appear? (He did not.) There was Monte Irvin, the glorious old Giant out-fielder. Would Bowie Kuhn, the Baseball Commissioner, arrive? (He did not.)

But the coffin *was* open. No chattering could obscure that for long and I looked at the leonine head of the young man newly dead. His beard was trimmed. For an instant I allowed myself to consider what was locked within the skull: Gibran and Her-bie Mann and racism and the faces of teen-aged Asians killed in battle and the narcosis of heroin and the shock of withdrawal and a father's hug. And then I would not let myself think that way any more.

The family was escorted to their pews at 1:15. Rachel Robin-son, who had mixed martinis with exquisite care when last we saw her, was clinging to another of her children. Two men had to support Jackie Robinson, most powerful of base runners. He was crying very softly for his son, his head down so that the tears coursed only a little way before falling to the floor.

A solo flute played "We Shall Overcome." A chorus from Daytop sang "Bridge over Troubled Water" and "Swing Low, Sweet Chariot." One is prepared for moving music at funerals, but then something happened that surprised everyone: Monte Irvin, Hugh Morrow, the people of the parish who twenty-five years ago had known the Robinson family as neighbors. David Robinson, who was nineteen, walked to the pulpit—with a wide stride—and read a eulogy for his brother. David had written it in a single afternoon and pleaded with his father to be allowed to speak it.

"He climbed high on the cliffs above the sea," David called in a resonant tenor, "and stripped bare his shoulders and raised his arms to the water, crying, 'I am a man. Give me my freedom so that I might dance naked in the moonlight and laugh with the stars and roll in the grass and drink the warmth of the sun. Give me my freedom so I might fly.' But the armies of the sea continued to war with the wind and raced through the stones and mocked his cries, and the man fell to his knees and wept."

David had finished a year at Stanford. Soon he would go off to travel Europe. Jackie Robinson, Jr. had intended to buy the yellow MG, helping David to a stake.

"He rose," David's voice called from the pulpit, "and journeyed down the mountain to the valley and came upon a village. When the people saw him, they scorned him for his naked shoulders and wild eyes and again he cried, 'I am a man. I seek the means of freedom.'

"The people laughed, saying, 'We see no chains on your arms. Go. You are free.' And they called him mad and drove him from their village." The man walked on, "eyes red as a gladiator's sword," until he came to a stream where he saw an image, face sunken in hunger, "skin drawn tight around the body.

"He stood fixed on the water's edge and began to weep, not from sorrow but from joy, for he saw beauty in the water and he removed his clothing and stood naked before the world and rose to his full height and smiled and moved to meet the figure in the water and the stream made love to his body and his soul cried with the ecstasy of being one."

Now David's hero recognized himself and David's strong voice rose and choired, "He laughed, for he felt the strength of the stream flowing through his veins, and he cried, 'I am a man,' and the majesty of his voice was heard above the roar of the sea and the howl of the wind, *and he was free.*"

David rushed from the pulpit. His mother rose to embrace him. Sobs rang through the old church; it was five minutes before formal worship resumed.

"Who was crying?" Jimmy DeJohn said later. "I just know one person. Me."

"Could have been anybody," Hugh Morrow said. "It could have made anybody cry."

But even as our small group drove back toward New York, wondering how to atone or make memorial, we had seen Jackie Robinson after the services, white-haired, dry-eyed and sure, as when he doubled home two runs, walking among street people outside the church, talking perhaps of the hell of heroin, touching and being touched, and we thought how proud his first-born son would have been, not of the ball player but of the man, had he lived, if only the insanity of the present had given him a chance.

II

Sixteen months later an autumn day broke with a dawn awakening. My wife, Alice, stood above the bed, her shoulders taut in tension, her lips pinched. "Jackie died. Channel 7 needs a telephone interview."

"What do you remember?" a poised announcer was asking easily.

"He was supposed to be here for a dinner party a week from Saturday. His doctors were concerned about his circulation. They asked him to start drinking. Jack was beginning with vodka and orange juice, and I'd been debating whether to load the first drink I was to be allowed to make him in twenty years of friendship."

"Interesting," the announcer said. "Now what would sum him up?"

"Courage. Humanity."

Then a condolence call at the stone house beside the bank of a reservoir that borders Stamford, Connecticut. A moment at the dark-wood doors with his son David. Choked, ghastly sobs. And then in rapid order someone else had planned, I found myself speaking six television tributes.

It is a lesson of Jackie Robinson's life that one meets challenge. But the process of repeatedly answering identical questions is dehumanizing. After a while you tend to remember your previous answer rather than the bar of music that was the man. "Courage and humanity," I heard myself saying over and over. "That's what Jackie Robinson was about."

When a friend dies, one is assaulted by shock. Emotions jumble into grief, fright and anger at death's omnipotence. The sense of human loss, the flowers of friendship faded, comes more slowly. Forever onward, one realizes gradually, this face, this voice, this vibrant form, will grow more dim. With Jackie Robinson, the estrangement was being accelerated by repetitive interviews.

My wife and I went to the funeral on a blue pass. There were blue passes for friends and buff passes for the press. Ushers led us through the engulfing cathedral of Riverside Church and into the private chapel where Jackie Robinson lay sealed in his coffin.

Rachel sat weeping and bent by her terrible grief. "I'm sorry, Rae," I said. I leaned to kiss her, and her tears touched my cheek. That benediction brought back the man that was.

When I met Robinson in the spring of 1952, I found a fierce, commanding gentleman, already a hero to many and as surely a threat to some. In the 1950s whites tended to like Negroes as Stepin Fetchit, if at all. Jackie Robinson did not have eyes that popped and he wasn't afraid of ghosts and he never said, "Yowsah, boss." "How the hell are you?" was his kind of greeting, in a clearly enunciated, ringing tenor.

The New York *Herald Tribune* had sent me to cover the Robinson Dodgers, the boys of summer in what George Frazier has called their youth and sinew; but as I rode the Pullmans on that first spring barnstorming tour, American racism was what stirred me. On the way to the ball game in Mobile, a white taxi driver complained that baseball had let in cannibals. At a dinner in Chattanooga, a minor league executive excoriated a waiter for misreading drink orders; every third word was "nigger." At the ball parks all the crowds were segregated and most of the rooting was ethnic. A Robinson foul tip, strike one, drew roars from the whites. A wide curve, ball one, drew cheers from blacks crammed into the farthest reaches of the grandstand. The taxis were segregated and the hotels were segregated and the restaurants were segregated, and on the streets of Southern towns, blacks stepped into the gutter to let the white bucks pass.

"I'm sure it doesn't mean a damn, Jack," I said, "but I just want you to know I think this racist stuff is a disgrace."

"Then write it."

"I will."

"You'll be the first."

"This must be hell."

Robinson was strong, with skin of ebony. His eyes could blaze. Now they laughed.

"Never been there," he said, and winked. And we were friends.

That was one twinkling of the man. The ball player strides through *The Boys of Summer:*

Robinson could hit and bunt and steal and run. He had intimidating skills and he burned with a dark fire. He wanted passionately to win. He charged at ball games. He calculated his rivals' weaknesses and measured his own strengths, and he knew—as only a few have known—the precise move to make at precisely the moment of maximum effect. His bunts, his steals, and his fake bunts and his fake steals humiliated a legion of visiting players. He bore the burden of a pioneer and the weight made him more strong. If one can be certain of anything in baseball, it is that we shall not look upon his like again.

He was outspoken, profane, sometimes shrill and always marvelous copy. He had opinions on almost everything, and if something he said turned out to be wrong, he never cried misquote. "Maybe I shouldn't have said it," you'd hear in those high tones, "but damn, I did."

Some of the press, like his teammates, had difficulty with his presence. "He's a pop-off," older newspapermen told me.

"And Leo Durocher, Eddie Stanky?"

"Oh, they're holler guys. You know, competitors."

"So's Robinson."

"No. He's a troublemaker."

Although no one recognized it at the time, this warrior on

racist plains was profoundly a nonviolent man. Although no one understood it then, this firebrand was imbued with old-fashioned, even Old World, values.

He decided to quit baseball before, not after, the Dodgers sold him to the Giants, treating a national hero as if he were a used car. He'd forged ten glorious years, six Dodger pennants, and the shattering of the barrier. Approaching forty, he was too much a realist to want the silver tarnished by limping seasons and base hits twice a week.

"There is no easy place for the old ball player in society," he was saying a few weeks before he died. Dick Young had written that he was embittered because he could not contribute so grandly to society after baseball as he had done in his playing years. Like despair, bitterness was alien to Jackie Robinson, but he did want to manage a major league team. When that was denied, he threw himself into business and politics.

We met from time to time and bantered. He was concerned, he said, that the Democratic party would always have to accommodate its Southern whites. That was an argument advanced by Wendell Willkie for Republicanism during the 1940s. Robinson innately felt comfortable with conservative arguments. His success had taken place within a system. He believed in capitalism, orderly integration and the American flag.

When Jack Junior began dangerous games with drugs, the family solution had him "straighten himself out by joining the Army." Long afterward, when young Jack careened off the Merritt Parkway in a sports car, I made the dread, obligatory telephone call.

"Can I do something?" I asked the father. "Call the papers?"

"Request that, instead of flowers, contributions go to fight drugs."

"Sure." Then silence. "Jack, I'm trying to say you have our love."

"You don't have to." The bereaved father's voice was strong. "By calling us, you already did."

Now in the big church sixteen months later, the Reverend Jesse Jackson interrupted a brilliant, hard eulogy, to speak softly of death: "He stole home."

"The hell he did," Irving Rudd, out of the old Brooklyn Dodger office, was storming afterward. "I knew the guy, and if there's a God, Jackie's up there now and he's ripped off his cap and he's kicking dirt with his spikes and he's hollering, 'What a lousy decision. I shoulda been safe. I was only fifty-three!' "

One cannot end with angry sorrow. During the summer of 1972, I hosted a luncheon at which Robinson was awarded a variety of gifts. As a final present, I said, concluding the affair, "We are not going to ask Jackie Robinson to make a speech."

A minute later he was calling my name. "Damn, I wish you had let me express my appreciation."

"Seemed best this way," I said, and bit a lip.

"Sure," Jack said, and then he thanked me with his eyes, and put that strong black hand on my forearm and squeezed; and it struck me how he met men and women not as black or white but as colleagues in mankind, and how through the fires of his life, some others came to do the same.

I can still feel that hand on my forearm.

Sleep well.

A Coffin for My Father

When the 1953 Brooklyn Dodgers, the best baseball team that I have seen, lost the World Series badly to the Yankees, I wrote an account of their sepulchral dressing room for the New York *Herald Tribune*. I had been covering the Dodgers for two years and it shocked me to see such poised and powerful men as Duke Snider and Jackie Robinson imprisoned by grief. It was unfair, I suggested, that the best team doesn't always get to win.

Jesse Abramson, the *Tribune*'s skillful, hard-boiled fight writer, said my story showed excessive emotional involvement. Bob Cooke, the sports editor, agreed. "Take a week off," Cooke said. "Get some perspective."

I read the newspapers. Nigel Bruce, the great Watson, died at fifty-eight, deserting his confederate, Rathbone-Holmes. Kathleen Ferrier, who made men weep as she sang Mahler's *Kindertotenlieder,* died of cancer at the age of forty-one. After Herbert Brownell, Jr., Attorney General to President Eisenhower, investigated the personal finances of Joe McCarthy, he cleared the Senator of breaking criminal statutes. That Wednesday night, as ever, I visited my parents for a resumption of our ritual reading of *Ulysses* according to my mother, Olga Kahn.

We tried the chapter in which Joyce describes the birth of Mina Purefoy's baby at 10 P.M., on June 16, 1904, the progress of the language and the development of the embryo coinciding in laborious labor. We drove through it for a listless hour, after which Olga prepared coffee.

"Well," said Gordon Kahn, my father, "at least you can't complain that it was an uninteresting baseball season. Your assignment certainly wasn't dull."

"No, but in the end I felt flat."

"Maybe you'd enjoy covering another club next year."

"I've got good sources on the Dodgers. I don't know if I could build up others as good and, anyway, going through the whole thing again would probably bore me."

"Suit yourself, but isn't twenty-five early to worry about boredom? By the way, the Erskine strikeout piece wasn't a bad story, not a bad piece of work at all." We both felt tired. After coffee Gordon saw me to the door. He was smoking a Pall Mall behind a long, bent ash. His gray eyes were soft, but the deep voice grated from a cold when he said, "Good night, chief."

The next day's newspapers broke the remarkable news that Charlie Dressen was through as manager of the Dodgers. Ruth Dressen had written a harsh letter to Walter O'Malley, the club president, demanding a three-year contract and O'Malley immediately invited Charlie to his office, at 215 Montague Street. He slapped Charlie's back, indicated a chair and said through a cigar, "Is what Ruth says what you feel you've got to have?"

"Yeah," Dressen said, averting his eyes.

"Then I think we should call a press conference for tomorrow morning. The policy here, as you know, Charlie, is one-year contracts. At the press conference we can announce together that you're leaving." Dressen blinked and shook his head. "Me and my wife got to have security," he said.

"Of course," O'Malley said. "I wouldn't try to hold you."

My vacation ended in time for me to follow up this remarkable story. Dressen's Dodgers had just won their second successive pennant. Now he was unemployed. We rode aimlessly through a morning in someone else's car and the manager filled my ear with brave talk about the future, bright memories of the past and obscenities. "You wasn't fucking bad, kid," he said, in a burst of warmth. "Shit, you wasn't fucking bad at all."

Back at the *Tribune,* I wrote a thousand words, describing Dressen's plans and suggesting that he would soon be back in the major leagues with another pennant winner. (He never was.) I wondered if this were to be the last story I'd write about him. Against that possibility, I took pains to recast his remarks into reasonable grammar and churchwarden English. I knew Charlie would appreciate that.

At home that night in my small apartment on Clinton Avenue in Brooklyn, I poured a drink and turned on the radio. A newscaster was talking about an espionage ring within the Signal Corps, "still operating, according to a close friend of Julius Rosenberg, executed atom spy." I didn't care. I looked forward to bouncing the Dressen experience off my father, who, for all his scholarship, shared Charlie's vital lunatic optimism. It would be cloudy tonight, the announcer said, with a low of 55 degrees. The Dressen experience, as I considered it, sounded like a title for a tract. The whole thing, the Dodger loss to the Yankees and the mousetrapping of their manager, possessed, it seemed as I poured a second drink, certain elements of tragedy.

The telephone rang. It was 6:35. "Are you sitting down?" my sister Emily began.

"Which one?"

"Dad."

"What? What's that? Was it at least quick?"

"They think so. He died on a sidewalk. There wasn't any doctor. They think it was a heart attack. Can you come over to Kings County Hospital? I'm taking care of Mother. They want someone to identify the body."

I drove down dark streets at reckless speed. The sidewalk was a rotten place to die. Pebbled cement scrapes a twitching face.

A man deserves privacy at the end, and anesthesia. Surely my father had earned that for a gentle life. Myself, ungentle, now must stand and call the corpse my father. Would they have stripped him naked? My father's final day on earth I had spent with Charlie Dressen. The dying gasp and grimace on cement. Oh, I hope someone has had the kindness to close the mouth.

Corpse consigned to a licensed mortician, municipal codes conformed to, the $7.52 Gordon had been carrying received and signed for, I guided my mother and sister back to the spacious apartment. We sat in the living room with the French doors and blue-gray walls. The apartment was too large now. Everything had shrunk: books, sounds, paintings, carpets, people. My father's supper waited in the dining room. A half grapefruit had been cut and sectioned. His blue water goblet had been filled.

"There shouldn't be a rabbi," Olga said. "He should have an agnostic's funeral."

"Sure," I said. But what the hell was that?

Olga's dark eyes bulged. She chattered ceaselessly. It was hard to comprehend that this small iron lady, my mother, was babbling.

"I want a cremation," she said.

That was sensible, Roman, un-Catholic and sensible. Olga sat on the blue couch, legs crossed, circular face controlled, except for the eyes. "My father was cremated," Olga said. "He was your grandfather, you know. Why don't you ever talk about your grandfather? Or write about him? He was a remarkable man. Many people would be interested in the story of his life. That is what you might write, instead of baseball, if you can. Papa's story. I want the two ashes, both urns, Daddy's and Papa's, side by side."

"I'll see about a cremation," I said.

"How can you cremate Daddy? Don't you know his favorite joke? When he died, he wanted to be cremated. Then, when a lover came to call some icy night, he said, I could scatter his ashes on the ice, so that my lover wouldn't fall and hurt himself." My mother's hands went to her face. The fingers spread and I saw, without hearing, the hands that once played simple Mozart duets with mine.

Joe Blau, an old associate of my father's who taught religion at Columbia, and led an Ethical Culture group, said he would handle the eulogy, asserting neither that there is a God nor that there is none.

"That's about where we are, Joe," I said.

"I suppose you're full of his favorite quotations."

"Sure." But I was not. I thought for a long time. Applesauce, he had said, and something about Dressen coming back with Erskine and something from *Caesar:* It seems to me most strange that men should fear, seeing that death, a necessary end, will come when it will come. But that was Shakespeare swelling a scene. "What I remember, Joe, is that he really liked the second movement of Beethoven's Seventh."

"I can think of many quotations," Joe Blau said with rabbinic solemnity. "Why don't you console yourself with one from Socrates? 'To a good man no evil can come either in life or after death.'"

When a father dies, a son buys a coffin, entering the mercantilism of mourning. Coffin salesmen are specialists at turning guilt into profit and as Simenon writes, "When someone is dead, you feel guilty, even if for a smile you did not smile."

A deluge of Gordon's frightened friends, thirty years older than I, and glad to have been spared, decided that lawyers should accompany me to the mortuary. Several lawyers vied for the place as, at certain parties where a girl is stricken, rival doctors contend to make the examination. Two lawyers prevailed. Intense, affluent Jack Lippman played good tennis and once at a lake of summer asked me, "Pitch in a few." Lippman wore eyeglasses and his swing was awkward. After he missed five times, I threw medium-speed high outside pitches. Lunging, he drove some to right field. I would never have thrown that way to my father; he'd have lined the ball back into my teeth. Silent, sorrowing Gus Simpson was a Socialist who had lost an eye in physical combat with followers of the Jew-baiting priest, Charles Coughlin. I drove to the mortuary with two men, physically flawed but living while my father, who could see perfectly and hit a baseball hard, lay wreathed in the faint odor of embalming fluid.

In brilliant, mild weather, I guided my pale-green car through the twisting roadway inside Prospect Park. The mortuary, a modest red-brick building, stood near the southwest corner, between a roller skating rink and the ball fields of the Parade Grounds which stretched for five hundred yards.

It was the morning of October 17. An expressionless man, wearing a dark suit, waited inside the mortuary door. "My office is this way," he said. He acknowledged the two lawyers. "Are these your uncles?"

"They're lawyers," I said.

"Burial is a private matter."

"We're here to talk price," Jack Lippman said, in a high, dry voice, "and we don't have very much time."

The mortician looked at Lippman. "Prices range up from four hundred dollars. The price of the coffin is the determining factor. Use of a chapel and one limousine are included. Was the deceased well-off?"

"No," Jack Lippman said.

"I'm buying the casket," I said.

"Yes," the mortician said to me. "We have excellent coffins for men of reasonable but not necessarily extensive means. Something with a copper lining for twelve hundred fifty will last for centuries. With that we include artificial grass, so that the area around the grave is consistent green."

"He's being cremated," I said.

"Where is this four-hundred-dollar coffin?" Lippman said.

"We'll take the twelve-fifty coffin," Simpson said. He fixed

Lippman coldly and said to me, "Gordon was a wonderful man. He deserves the best."

The mortician led us into a softly lighted showroom in which an air conditioner whined. Coffins stood everywhere on sturdy bases: dark, carefully rubbed fruitwoods, with white cloth lining; dull, handsome copper; plain pine for Orthodox Jews. The prices, except for the plain pine, exceeded $1,000.

"Where's the four-hundred-dollar one?" Lippman said.

The mortician pressed his lips and sighed. He opened a door and walked into another room. Here coffins were tightly stacked on shelves. "That," he said, indicating a coffin covered with gray cloth.

"We'll take it," Lippman said.

I walked to the cloth coffin and touched it. This was my father's coffin; then at last, I had come to the coffin one removed from my own. I withdrew my hand. The cloth beneath was darker. The shade was sensitive to moisture, touch, life. Five hundred people coming to the funeral and I had bought a coffin of chameleon gray.

"No," Gus Simpson said. "That just won't do."

I walked toward a fruitwood coffin marked $685. "This one," I said.

"Do you wish time payments?"

"I've got the money."

"Shall I notify the newspapers?"

"I've taken care of that."

I followed the mortician back to his office, and while Jack Lippman and Gus Simpson ignored each other's glares, I signed a funeral contract, which I discovered two weeks later included $15 extra for artificial grass. Was it artificial fescue? I wondered. Was Merion more?

Outside a summer sun was taunting. I walked to the car, a lawyer at each elbow, wholly alone. The wrongness of things seized me. At the Parade Grounds boys were throwing footballs. It was that season; baseball would come again. The team was broken up and with my father dead there was no one with whom I wanted to consider that tragedy, and because there was no one I recognized that the breaking of a team was not like greater tragedy: incompleteness, unspoken words, unmade music, withheld love, the failure ever to sum up or say good-bye.